PUṢPA

Puṣpa

A photographic essay in which cut flowers are coupled
with Indian and south-east Asian sculptures and reliefs

Compiled and photographed by ORNAN ROTEM

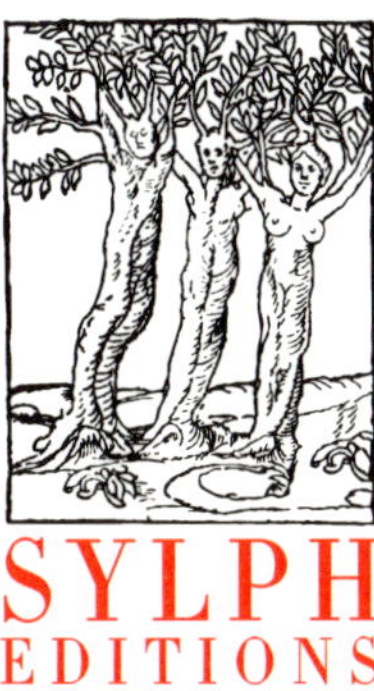

SYLPH
EDITIONS

For Num, the reason for it all

Es gibt eine zarte Empirie, die sich mit dem Gegestand innigst macht, und dadurch zur eigentlichen Theorie wird.

There is a form of tender empiricism that makes itself so intimate with its object that it thereby becomes proper theory.

From *Wilhelm Meisters Wanderjahre, oder Die Entsagenden* (1821)
by JOHANN WOLFGANG VON GOETHE
quoted by WALTER BENJAMIN,
quoted in turn by JOHN BERGER

Numinous connections

Preamble

This book is a photographic essay in which classical Indian and south-east Asian sculptures and reliefs, mostly originating in the first millennium of the Common Era, are juxtaposed with photographs of cut flowers. Prima facie, this coupling might seem somewhat odd or perhaps merely quaint, since there is nothing obvious to tie the two together. The flowers are natural organic forms while the sculptures are stone, terracotta, stucco and ivory artifices formed by the skilled hands of anonymous artisans. The flowers are alive, of the moment, their allotted span traversing days; the sculptures are very much of the past: inanimate, frozen as it were, hundreds of years ago. The flowers display themselves in colourful exuberance while the sculptures, as we have them, are seemingly impassive and monochromatic. Both exude beauty – each in its own way – but does this in itself merit placing them alongside one another?

There are two ways to address this question: the first is to remain silent and to let the couples speak for themselves, let them perform and let the spectator be convinced, or not, by the performance. This drama is the heart of this book. It is also possible to attempt to ground the praxis in theory, which is what follows.

1 *The flowery nature of the sculptures and the sculptural quality of flowers*

One of the most striking features of the venerable and occasionally crumbling sculptures portrayed in this book is that when seen in the flesh one is struck by their vibrancy, so much so that the word 'flesh' breaks loose from the realm of metaphor. One is tempted to say that they are endowed with life. In the main, these sculptures and reliefs depict celestial and earthly figures who abound in character and exude emotion. Their subtle gestures, their charged expressions and their nuanced physique are set in a solidity that seems to shimmer with every gaze, with every passing ray of light. The different angles from which one can gaze at a sculpture combined with the play of light and shadow makes them dynamic and fluid and the sum of one's observation is, in effect, a moving picture – in both senses of the word: affective and kinetic.

Most of the ancient stone sculptures we see today are predominantly mono-chromatic even though in their original state they would have been brightly painted and decorated. Extant Egyptian sculptures, on account of favourable climatic conditions, retain their brilliant original colours, but Greek and Roman

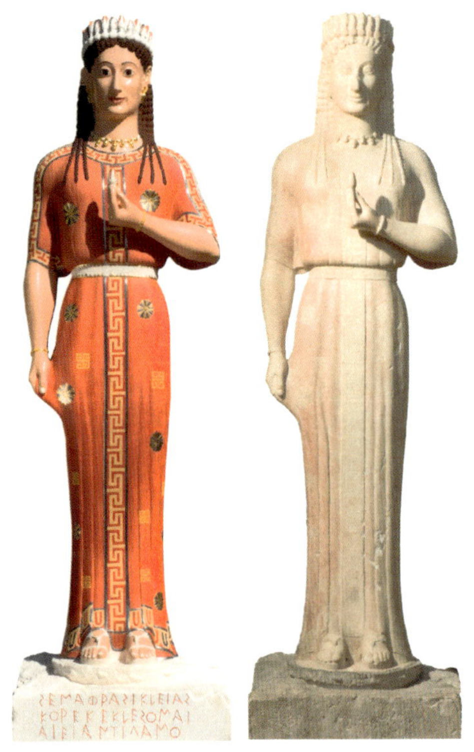

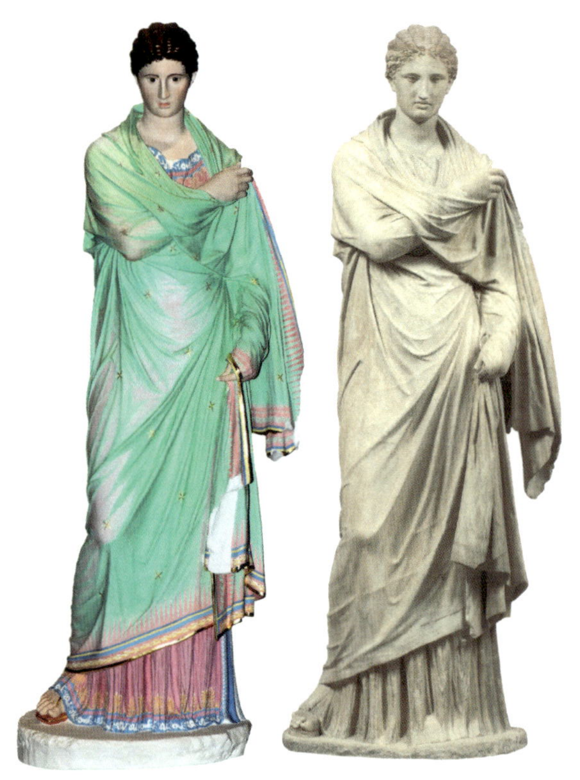

Colour reconstruction of original Greek sculptures by Vinzenz Brinkmann and Ulrike Koch-Brinkmann from the exhibition Gods in Colour, *first shown in 2008 at the Liebieghaus Skulpturen Sammlung in Frankfurt.*

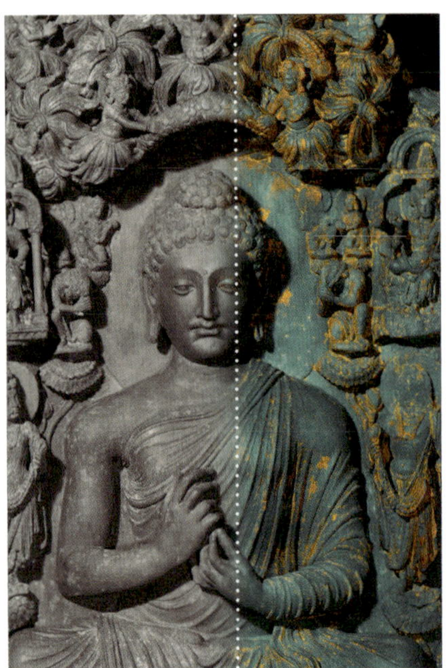

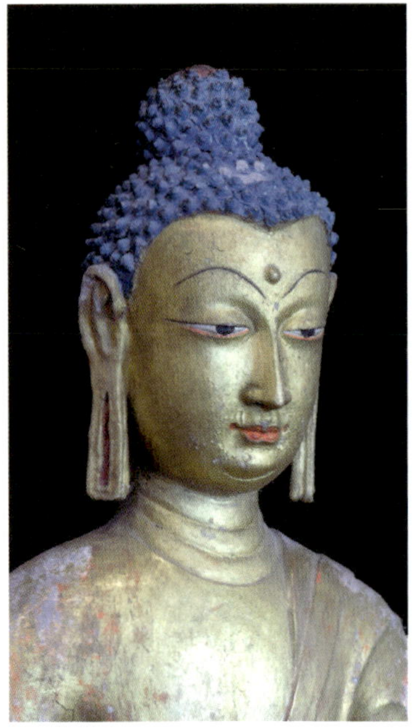

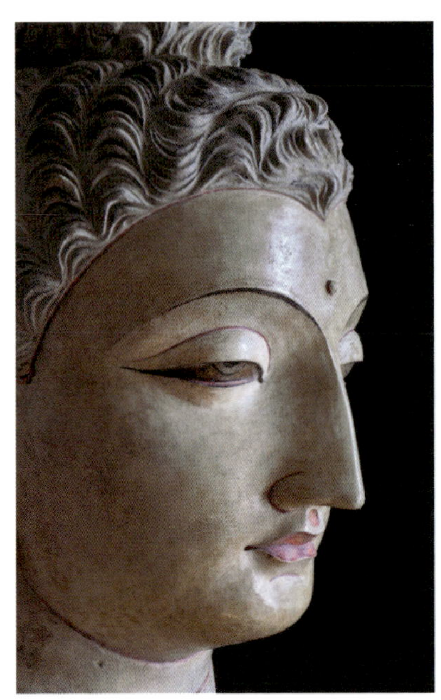

Photographic colour-spectrum analysis highlighting residual gilding on a detail of a 4th-century Gandhāran relief (right) compared to the same (left) presented monochromatically; reproduced on pages 50-51.

Gilding and colouring on a 15th-century seated Buddha, made of clay composite and originating in Western Tibet; reproduced on page 28.

Original colouring on 4th/5th-century Gandhāran stucco Buddha head; reproduced on page 83.

marbles have lost their polychromy because the painted layer was not as durable
as its substratum, and to confound things, when unearthed they were usually
scrubbed clean. This allowed them to conform to the aesthetic and intellectual
ideals developed in the Renaissance that favoured a supposed purity of form
articulated in the idea of whiteness (in passing one should note that this resonated
with the West's attempts to justify the myth of racial superiority, especially in the
19th and 20th centuries). So prevalent was the predilection for white that even a
sensitive humanist such as Goethe, to whom we shall return later, succumbed to
it, saying that 'savage nations, uneducated people and children have a great predilection for vivid colours.' However, the oft-denied polychromy of the sculptures
was always evident for those willing to see it. Contemporary research is supplying
verifiable analysis of the exact colour and specific techniques used in antiquity
and today there is a tendency among curators to emphasize and demonstrate
polychromy in exhibitions by means of reliable reconstructions, so much so that
sometimes classic sculptures, celebrated for their finesse and refinement, end up
being dressed in unpalatable garish colours looking both vulgar and tacky (by our
standards, of course). One of the more tasteful curatorial techniques employed
is the video projection of colour onto originals that enables us to see the works
as they are now, that is colourless, and then how they would have been at their
time, that is in full colour. For example, in its 2018 exhibition *I am Ashurbanipal*, the
British Museum convincingly applied this method on several Assyrian reliefs, but
curiously the 350-page book accompanying the exhibition that amply reproduced
the reliefs did not show them polychromatically even once. In most cases Indian
and south-east Asian sculptures would have been adorned with colour and not
infrequently gilded. Some of the pieces in this book not made of stone, such as the
stucco Gandhāran Buddha on page 83 or the clay Tibetan Buddha on page 28, have
retained their original colourings while others, such as those in ivory or terracotta,
may not have been painted at all.

Tastes change slowly and modernists are still very much attached to classic
images of 'pure' ancient works, relishing their (inauthentic) achromaticism. The
photographs in this book wilfully adhere to this aesthetic; rendering the objects in
black and white not only conforms to our hallowed expectations but, unwittingly,
perhaps, reinforces our collective blindness to polychromy. Jan Stubbe Østergaard,
who put on two exhibitions at Copenhagen's Glyptotek that featured colour
reconstructions of classical sculptures, reports that many visitors objected to what
he questionably calls a 'necessary evil'. This book approaches the 'necessary evil'
differently: it relishes the joys of the conformist monochromatic aesthetics and
then undermines it by adding colour circuitously – but more on that to follow.

Puṣpa (पुष्प), pronounced '*pushpa*', is Sanskrit for 'flower'. In some respects, flowers
are the diametric opposite of the hardy sculptures; they are organic, evanescent,
colourful and with very little evident interference of human agency or design.

Flowers and the inorganic materials from which the sculptures are formed inhabit very different time realms; flowers epitomize transience while stone and its like embodies endurance. However, if one delves deeper it is possible to see that they have more in common than initially meets the eye and, moreover, juxtaposing the two on a spread in a book suggests that they can meaningfully inform one another.

Consider for example their respective relationship to temporality. The sculptures endure; no little part of the fascination they hold for us is the manner in which they embody entropy. They are no less beautiful to us if they are broken, spoilt, or if they acquire the patina of age and other marks of decay and impermanence. This internal dialogue between the artwork and its material, between its long-forgotten creator and the timeless ideas this creator was trying to convey, is one of the cornerstones of our appreciation of these works. But the sculptures were not created merely to please or to entertain, they are objects of contemplation and the aesthetics underlying them is of a devotional nature. These works were created in order to edify, to embody a story or to portray a character that stands for ideas and cardinal principles that, in turn, embody a whole teaching or an entire cosmological outlook. Many of the works in this book are Buddhist, a key tenet of which is the teaching that all conditioned existence is marked by impermanence (*anitya*), that all is transient and in a state of flux. Another prominent idea carved into the sculptures originating in India is the cyclical cosmology of birth and rebirth (*saṃsāra*), a fundamental assumption about the nature of the world in classical India. These ideas – transience, impermanence, a cycle of regeneration – are temporal in nature and notwithstanding their doctrinal complexity, the juxtaposition with flowers offers powerful visual cues since transience, impermanence and regeneration are among the most obvious characteristics of flowers. It is as if looking at the sculptures through the prism of the flowers loosens the grip temporality has on them, allowing them to be read like writing in the sand rather than inscriptions in stone.

There is another interesting and perhaps subliminal crossover. In order to edify and to function devotionally, sculptures must attract. Without this attraction it would not be possible to engage with them in a way that would engender the desired deeper or more meaningful understanding of the world. This is prominent in Buddhist sculptures and reliefs, whose purpose is to create an engaged dialogue and it can be applied unquestionably to most of the other works in this book (though admittedly about some we have scant information). These engagements are procreative, their issue is knowledge, and beyond that, knowledge that will ultimately endow the devotee with wisdom. Similarly, the role of flowers in nature is first to attract, then to engage and for this biological engagement to beget new form, though plainly with little regard to humans. We are, to put it crudely, mere bystanders, witnesses to sexual reproduction; we are but voyeurs relishing the engagement of flower and pollinator (and in the case of non-sexual reproduction, self-pollination).

There is also a more mundane sense in which one can argue that flowers in this context have a sculptural quality: they are very often present in the sculptures themselves. This is not a decorative coincidence: flowers in Indian culture occupy a prominent place, be it in cosmology, iconography and mythology, or in literature, poetry and doctrine. Consequently, it is only natural that they will be an essential part of the sculptures' grammar. This is plainly evident when one embarks on a bee's eye view of one of India's most cherished flowers – the lotus or *padma* (for which there are dozens of evocative synonyms in Sanskrit, not so surprising given the importance of the lotus and the inherent word-building capabilities of Sanskrit).

Let us begin, then, at the beginning, at a beginning, since creation is cyclical. Viṣṇu is sleeping on the primal waters of the vast shoreless ocean of nothingness during the night of all nights, reclined within the endless coils of the thousand-headed serpent called the Ananta (Endless). The whole universe is folded within Viṣṇu as primordial form, like an unborn babe. The world begins afresh when from the Supreme Being's navel a thousand-petalled lotus of pure gold emerges, on top of which sits Brahmā who will duly split the flower into three and thereby bring the world into existence.

Some tell it differently, laying emphasis on the cosmic lotus that has always been associated with water, the female aspect of the universe. Though there is no explicit mention of a Lotus Goddess in the *Ṛg Veda*, the earliest of the sacred texts, it has been suggested that in the pre-Aryan cities of Mohenjo-daro and Harappa the feminine was actually supreme, attested to by extant depictions of a bare-breasted goddess with lotuses decking her hair. This goddess, or goddesses, may have trickled down to the predominantly patriarchal Vedic culture where we encounter divine consorts such as Umā and Lakṣmī (pages 70 and 60), associated in every possible way with the lotus. One possible manifestation of this could be the lotus-headed goddess known as Lajjā Gaurī mostly depicted with exposed genitalia (see page 45).

Were all the symbols of the world to convene in one place, and were the Buddhist traditions throughout the ages to lay claim to one symbol, it would undoubtedly be the lotus. To begin, again, at the beginning, let us recall one of its most prominent stories, the life story of Siddhārtha Gautama, the last Buddha. Prior to his birth, his mother, the great Queen Māyā, dreamed of a white bull elephant carrying a white lotus in its trunk; after his birth he took seven steps and immediately lotus flowers sprang underneath his feet. After enlightenment he likened himself to a lotus born in the water, grown in the water, rising up above the water, undefiled. He teaches the Dharma because, he says, like lotus flowers rising above muddy waters, some will understand him. Over time, his 'perfected wisdom' (*Prajñāpāramitā*) is represented by means of the lotus symbol and among the most important of ensuing bodhisattvas is Avalokiteśvara, many a time appearing as Padmapāṇi, 'Lotus-in-hand' (see page 76). It comes then as no surprise that the Buddha is customarily depicted sitting on a lotus throne.

2   *A marriage proposal*

What then happens to sculptures and flowers, this unlikely couple, when they are married by the powers vested in photography and the printed page? This is an arranged marriage, if there ever was one, and the dazzling melodramas of Indian cinema forever remind us how precarious such marriages will be unless they are blessed by the gods, whence love will prevail. The duty-bound elders must ensure the suitability of the match and as long as doubt lingers, they must object and hold forth.

Auntie is wary; she reminds us that the groom is austere, scholarly and steeped in tradition and a bride such as this, fickle, fanciful and frivolous, does not befit him. Marry him to an annotated sacred text, and if none can be found, to a learned dissertation with scholarly references and abundant footnotes. Another auntie also has her doubts, albeit of a different character: 'what do we know about the bride?' she asks, and then, without further ado, answers: 'She's been seen basking in the company of nudes, embracing poetry and lounging flirtatiously in fashion magazines … need I say more?'

This may all be incontrovertible, the matchmaker says, but the apparent incongruity is superficial. Deep down – where it matters – the couple share the same values and the marriage will bring these qualities to the fore, allowing them to form a harmonious and mutually beneficial bond.

Not readily convinced, a much-loved uncle on the bride's side is disquieted by the fact that the groom's substance is measured in geological time, while hers dances to the hours hand of a clock. He has eternity as his element, the duration of her life cycle is but nought in comparison and this mismatch will spell trouble. A suspicious cousin is worried about what he calls 'effusive outbursts of emotive colours' that, he says, are in her nature, and if we recognize and respect the groom's current achromaticism – regardless of what he may have been in his youth – we should nip this marriage in the bud. Considering himself a scholar of sorts, the objections put forward by this meddlesome relative resort to florid expressions such as his claim that the bride's 'emotive gestures are indicative of a desire drenched in melancholia that nervously oscillates between the two irreconcilable extremes of libido and thanatos', which means, in simple language, that she happily attends both weddings and funerals.

The matchmaker carefully listens to the concerns of the families. What follows is part summary and part expansion of his tortuous reply.

3   *The vexed issue of colour*

What exactly is colour? he asks; and what do we mean when we say that the sculptures are achromatic while the flowers are polychromatic? At its most basic it means that if we bring the two to a laboratory and measure their relative colour dispersion, the instruments will show a much larger variance among the flowers. However, it could be argued that while the reading is empirically valid it suffers from a certain

circularity since it is merely measuring the measurable. Colour should not be
thus reduced; conceptually there is more going on, hence the need to readdress
the age-old problem of whether colour is a quality of the physical world, hence
objective, or a token of the perceiving mind, hence subjective.

The answer, put succinctly, is that it is both. As a physical phenomenon colour
is merely a name we give to a particular segment of the spectrum of electromagnetic radiation (and a very small segment at that) which we refer to as 'visible
light'. Electromagnetic radiation is energy propagated through space in form
of waves, classified by their length (λ) and frequency (Hz) and in that respect
colour *as such* does not exist in the physical world. The

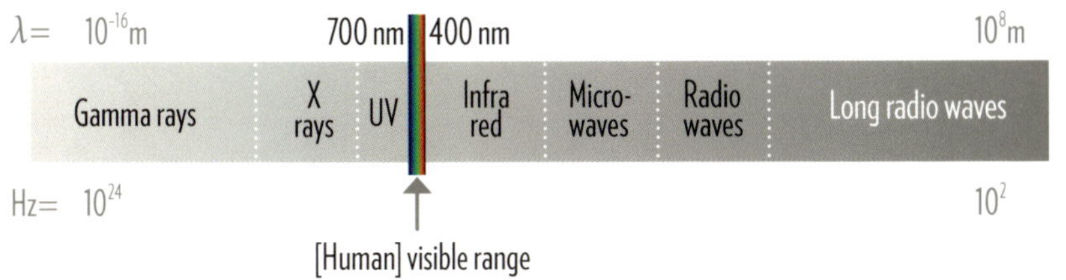

experience of colour arises when electromagnetic waves are perceived by the eye
and then transmitted through the optic nerve to the brain, which codifies these
sensations. Colour is grounded in external reality but is a singularly mental event.
Each colour we see consistently arises from the perception of a physical property
that exists independently of us; however, the experience of colour is a feature
of a brain process and thus prone to variation between species and individuals.
Dogs, fireflies and owls see the visible range differently, as do individuals within
the species.

Auntie is nervously shuffling in her seat.

4   *Goethe's koan*

The subtle distinction between objective and subjective means that we can
approach the experience of colour from two different angles: the empirical-
mechanistic approach, typically exemplified by Newtonian science and associated
with his and subsequent works on optics; but we can also embrace a different
kind of approach, it too claiming the right to be called scientific, namely, that
exemplified by Goethe and enunciated in his famous book *Zur Farbenlehre*, first
published in 1810. Admittedly, scientists of the first group do not think of
the latter as science at all. Although Goethe is best known as a poet, he also
studied, wrote and made meaningful and rarely challenged contributions
in the field of botany, geology, meteorology and zoology. His professed aim
was to integrate poetic and scientific sensibilities in order to provide a richer
understanding of the world based on a mode of inquiry that seeks to eliminate
the subject/object dualism, creating thereby a more delicate or tender form of
empiricism (*zarte Empirie*). His encyclopædic *Zur Farbenlehre* — 1,400 pages in

three volumes – is his most substantial work on colour and the sum of two decades of research. Since its publication it has been the object of intellectual scrutiny by artists, historians and philosophers. Ludwig Wittgenstein's penultimate work, *Remarks on Colour*, is a book-length meditation on the use of language in relation to colour that was spurred by a reading of Goethe. While Wittgenstein was intrigued by its scope, he rightly noted that 'Goethe's teaching of the constitution of colours of the spectrum has not proved to be an unsatisfactory theory, rather it really isn't a theory at all'. It is curious that *Zur Farbenlehre* has been consistently referred to in English as *Theory of Colours*, a misleading translation (probably originating with the title of the 1840 English edition) since '*Lehre*' is better conveyed by the term 'teaching.' This is not a quibble over words: the whole point of Goethe's position is that it is not a theory. However, it is wrong to think that just because it is not a (traditional scientific) theory then it must be some ineffectual and vapid opposite: an unprovable belief, a mystical insight, a poetic exposition. Goethe considered himself an empirical scientist; here and elsewhere he presents his findings based on strict reproducible observation. However, the purpose of this empiricism, the 'tender empiricism' as he called it, is not to partake in theory – its purpose is to induce in the observer a subtle understanding, a state of mind, if you will, that is so complete it not only renders a theory redundant, but causes the object of contemplation itself to become a 'theory' of sorts; or in his words:

> There is a form of tender empiricism that makes itself so intimate
> with its object that it thereby becomes proper theory.

Another way of putting it is to say that the role of traditional science is to dismantle the world and to do this by being objective, by obliterating the influence of the observer; Goethe is suggesting a science that after carefully dismantling the world, reassembles it by obliterating the subject/object division, effectively placing the observer at the centre. His critics say this is not science, though the more charitable view would be, perhaps, to call it a psychology.

Auntie is not among the charitable. She thinks the matchmaker has gone astray and plainly tells him so, while attempting to secure the support of the other auntie who has, alas, fallen asleep.

The matchmaker is not perturbed. He suggests we should treat this oft-quoted claim as a koan. The overly-learned cousin, not wanting to be outsmarted and forever seeking an opportunity to effuse, intervenes. He puts forward what he claims is a sensible proposal that, so he contends, might spur the investigation and avert thereby an impasse: 'would not this honourable assembly accumulate meritorious gains by grounding all these strange and obtuse ideas in verifiable colour practice? May I remind us all that an impending union is in the offing; wearisome meanderings and lamentable procrastinations might induce the pair to elope and expose them to a fate alarmingly similar to that of those Veronese star-crossed lovers of yore.'

And yet, the matchmaker resumes his discourse. There are, he says, considerable differences between Newtonian colour theory – which, with modifications, is the prevailing scientific theory – and Goethe, but since we all seem to be in a hurry, we shall concentrate on what is most pertinent to this affair. Firstly, as noted above, Newton is interested in establishing an analytical and mathematically valid theory of colour that excludes the perceiving eye; Goethe, on the other hand, is interested in integrating the physics of colour with the act of perceiving it, the experience of colour. Secondly, for Newton colourless light (often called mistakenly 'white light') is the sum of all colours and consequently darkness, in this scheme, is merely the absence of light. Black and white, darkness and light are immaterial to the theory. How is this demonstrated? Imagine a darkened chamber, and then make a small aperture through which a source of bright light enters, for example the sun. The ray of light penetrates this chamber and if there is nothing to obstruct it, nothing will be seen. Now obstruct its path with a triangular dispersive prism and if you place it at a very specific angle, and if you add a reflective surface on the opposing wall, you will see that the beam of light has fanned out into a spectrum of colours, with blue-violet at one end, red at the other and green in between. The conclusion is that visible light, 'white light', is comprised of an infinite number of colours spread out spectrally. Most importantly, Newton's genius was to show that these colours can, with the aid of another prism, be reassembled into white light. Newton chooses to 'see' seven basic colours – and why an asymmetric seven? Because the rainbow is a sign of cosmic harmony and so there must be seven, like the seven notes of the diatonic scale, and so he adds as basic colours orange and indigo (which before him was never regarded as a colour). To say this is a bit forced is an understatement and most colour practices prefer symmetric systems, i.e. a colour wheel of six: red, green, blue-violet (RGB) and their intermediaries: cyan, magenta, yellow (CMY).

Goethe arrives on the scene some hundred years later. Following Newton, he takes a prism but he doesn't begin with a darkened chamber. He places the prism to his eye and looks at a window through which sunlight is streaming in (diagrams 1 and 2). The transparent glass is bursting with light, the silhouetted frame and the glazing bars sectioning the pane are tenebrous. He instantly discovers something that he claims Newton completely missed. When you look *through* the prism, not *at* a prism, you see on the cusp – on the border between darkness and light – the appearance of two colours: yellow and blue, each of which intensifies towards the edges. These are the so-called 'boundary spectra' (a and b in diagram 2). Incidentally, this is much easier to demonstrate than Newton's fanning out colours and anyone with a prism observes this phenomenon straight away. Goethe concludes that colour, *pace* Newton, is not *in* light, but in the boundary *between* light and dark. If you then tilt the prism so that two adjacent boundary spectra merge (c in diagram 3), Newton's RGB appears, which leads

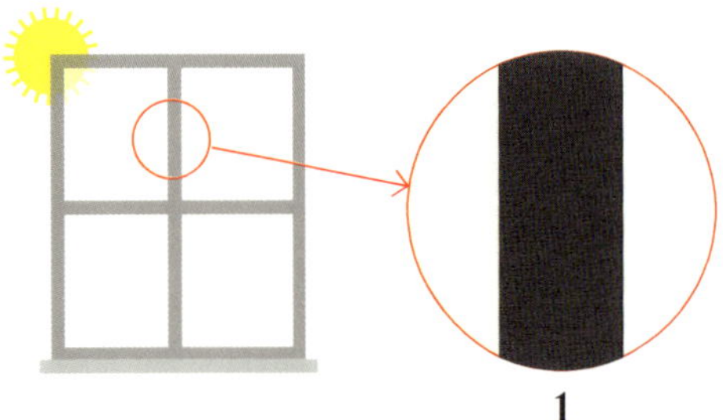

1

*Looking at a sunlit window pane
with the glazing bar (the muntin) silhouetted.*

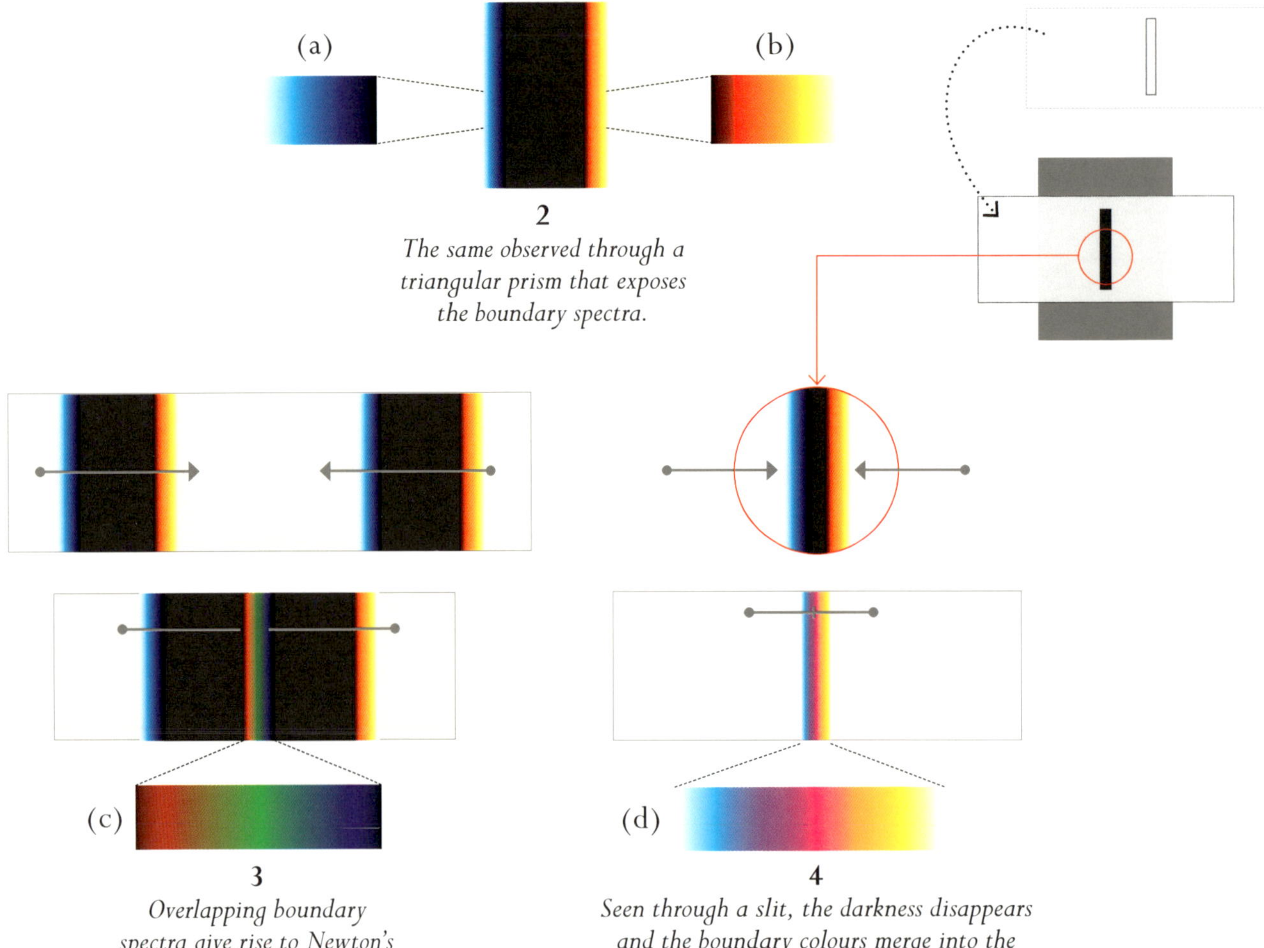

(a)   (b)

2

*The same observed through a
triangular prism that exposes
the boundary spectra.*

(c)

3
*Overlapping boundary
spectra give rise to Newton's
red-green-blue spectrum.*

(d)

4
*Seen through a slit, the darkness disappears
and the boundary colours merge into the
complimentary colours cyan, magenta and yellow.*

Goethe to say that Newton's RGB spectrum is a particular instance of a much broader phenomenon. Next, he explores the reverse: the previously dark surface is now bright, and the bright is dark. To do this, one holds a bright surface with a small slit against a relatively dark background. If the slit is narrow enough, the boundary colours will merge (d in diagram 4) and the complimentary colours cyan, magenta and yellow appear; thus we have identified Goethe's four spectra (a, b, c and d). The implication of this observation, from his point of view, is immense, since it gives rise to a wholly different understanding and application of colour. He then addresses colour along its physiological, physical, chemical properties and, famously the aesthetics, psychology and practical use of colour both in art and in architecture. One could say that his work is an inter-disciplinary, encyclopædic inventory of colour, but let us consider

here just a few of his insights, only those pertinent to the argument being put
forward, since in its totality Goethe's concept of colour is far beyond the scope of
prenuptial inquisitions.

If colour is seen as arising from the mixture between lightness and darkness,
darkness is not the absence of light, a nothing, but an essence, and that something
can be seen. Seen thus, are not cast shadows instances of visible darkness
demonstrated by our ability to perceive this grey as different hues? Goethe
contends that the sky, to mention another example, is also visible darkness. Beyond
the atmosphere there is complete darkness and so looking into a turbid medium
such the earth's atmosphere is to gaze at boundary spectra: at dawn and dusk,
facing the sun we see the red boundary spectrum and facing the other direction
we see the blue boundary spectrum, an astronomical repetition of diagram 2.

Herein lies the crux. Can we perhaps say that monochromatic representations
of achromatic sculptures and reliefs are actually colourful? Lets us return
momentarily to Goethe's koan: the first element is 'tender empiricism'. Hardy
empiricism registers no colour, but the soft empiricism we have been considering
suggests that these images in black and white are representations of light and dark
and hence the very source of colour and our whole chromatics. The eye as an
optic organ does not register these colours, but the mind is not limited to hardy
empiricism, especially, as we have seen, in the case of colours, and so is more
susceptible to the latent presence of a chromaticism of a different order. In his
koan, Goethe refers to this connection with the object as 'intimate', which is very
apt. It implies that to see these sculptures this way we need to feel close to them,
we need to feel connected and befriended. The juxtaposition with the flowers in
this instance is merely an attempt to make the intimate knowledge visible.

Since we are talking about marriage and presumably about love, the matchmaker, by way of illustration, brings as witness René Groebli's celebrated photo-
book *The Eye of Love,* being none other than intimate photographs celebrating
Rita, Groebli's wife, on their Paris honeymoon in 1952. Consider the following
perceptive lines that the curator Daniel Blochwitz wrote in his introduction to
The Magic Eye, a recent book celebrating Groebli's work:

> Groebli tirelessly probed the potential of his medium, seeking to
> record on photographic paper what the retina cannot capture. He
> did not aspire to perfecting vision, even less to objectivity; he aimed
> to counteract visual assumptions and enable us to perceive time and
> light, place and mood.

And through this intimacy, the empirical encounter with the object becomes
proper theory. This is the most puzzling aspect of Goethe's koan. What does
it mean for the experience of an object to become a theory, namely to see
monochromatic photographs of sculptures through the flowers' colour prism

and for this to be theory? To put it succinctly, though perhaps no less obscurely, the colours that the flowers expose turn the juxtaposition into a map.

The best way to explicate this, as above, is by analogy. The map I have in mind is a cosmogram, or in Sanskrit a *maṇḍala*. The cosmogram is a map of the universe, which can be understood in any number of ways, all depending on the theoretical framework in which it is employed. Unlike a regular map which represents the world, a section of the world, or a feature of it, the cosmogram is conceived of as a map that through certain practices, usually meditative, can be penetrated. For example, an architectural cosmogram is entered physically. The great Borobudur Stūpa in Java clearly demonstrates this, since it simultaneously represents Buddhist cosmology and the nature of the mind. The central stūpa, the sacred realm and the seat of Vairocana Buddha flanked by his four emanations, is not visible from ground level. As you enter the structure you begin to see the sculpted reliefs representing the world of desire, working your way up toward an inaccessible, but meaningful, empty centre. Being neither a temple nor a place of worship, it is a 'gigantic antenna that gathers forces and thoughts, condensing them into a lesson that pilgrims learn by degrees.'

From our point of view, the important feature that needs to be stressed when suggesting a cosmogram as an analogy is that the object of contemplation, when experienced intimately, transpires within a theoretical framework or, in other words, becomes theory.

6   *Ella-June Henrard's brimming carnality*

It would be wrong to say that the families are convinced: wearied, yes; exasperated, quite; baffled, more than they care to admit; but convinced, no. With most everyone longingly eyeing the cold buffet, the matchmaker, in an emotional plea, begs for their indulgence so that he may make a final exhortation, well worth repeating in full. This then is what he said, edited for clarity and concision.

'Some pages ago we solemnly gathered to see whether the powers vested in photography and printed form could sanction this strange union. By way of summation, I want to call up the testimony of expert witnesses; I could have – I would have – called three score, but as time is short, I'll settle for three.

'Anyone acquainted with the history of photography will appreciate the impact Irving Penn has had on photographing flowers. In a body of work spanning some four decades he managed to consistently "show flowers without showing off" (David Campany). One is tempted to say that it is the pollinator's point of view, the story of an agent of fertility that so identifies with its mission that it becomes seduced itself. Penn's colourful studies, shot against a white background, detach the flowers from all context; in one respect they are like the drawings of the great botanists of the previous centuries, drawings in which the self-imposed reticence of scientific observation begrudgingly erupts into art. Yet at the same time they are the exact opposite of the botanists' drawings if the latter are construed as an attempt to capture a representation of a species, a prototype. Each and every one of Penn's flowers is an individual; one feels he treats them as characters and that his photographs should be treated on a par with his portraits since each picture captures the flower's uniqueness and a very particular moment in its life cycle. Some flowers are fresh, radiant, young, while others are withered, decaying and at times even dismembered – but they are all personae in the great drama of life, ours and theirs.

'I call my next witness: F. L. Kenett and his photographs in the four-volume *Acanthus History of Sculpture*. Published in the early 1960s, the series covers Greek, Egyptian, Oceanic and Gothic sculpture. The books were published by the Oldbourne Press and printed impeccably in Lausanne in enviable black and white photogravure. Kenett did to sculpture what Penn did to flowers: create the impression of having done nothing special and turning that nothing into something exceptional. Without attention-seeking drama and suffused with humility he managed to show so much more than just dead matter. His tool box was limited to light and placement (which in the case of reliefs was converted into judicious cropping). Kenett chooses his placements humbly and lights the pieces without fanfare. The torso of the draped Nefertiti at the Louvre is set at a slight angle against a muted grey background with gently raking light that accentuates the texture of her drapery's clinging pleats (calling to mind the present-day "wet look"). The key light casts a slight shadow on the protrusions of her body: the small breasts, the elongated downward facing navel, the expectant stomach and triangular pubes. Were one to move around the piece in its actual setting, it would be up to the sculptor to make it speak; the photographer needs to retell the story by choosing only one of many possible vantage points and one light setting. Kenett's photograph has made the sculpture the story of a radiating queen, a royal spouse.

'The final witness I summon is a group of images in Marc Lagrange's collection *Senza Parole,* his last project before his untimely death in 2015. This group was shot in Tuscany, in Pietrasanta and Carrara, celebrated for their fine marble quarries and famous workshops that have been producing stone sculptures for centuries. Lagrange, well-known for his evocative and stylized fashion shoots, photographed nudes in the towns' dusty workshops and on location. The nudes appear in and among whitened sculptures and this creates a striking tension, a frisson brought about by the creative coupling of inanimate hard stone with vivacious nudes. Part of what makes these images interesting is that even when the models are completely covered in white dust and pose like sculptures, they are still unmistakeably alive. One image in particular is pertinent here: a double portrait of the actress Ella-June Henrard embracing an unnamed stone-like head. This portrait harks back to Man Ray's iconic *Noire et blanche,* 1926, in which Kiki de Montparnasse, her head resting on a table with eyes closed, props up an arresting African ebony mask. Lagrange has titled this image *Alto Rilievo* (*High relief*) and of all the images in the collection

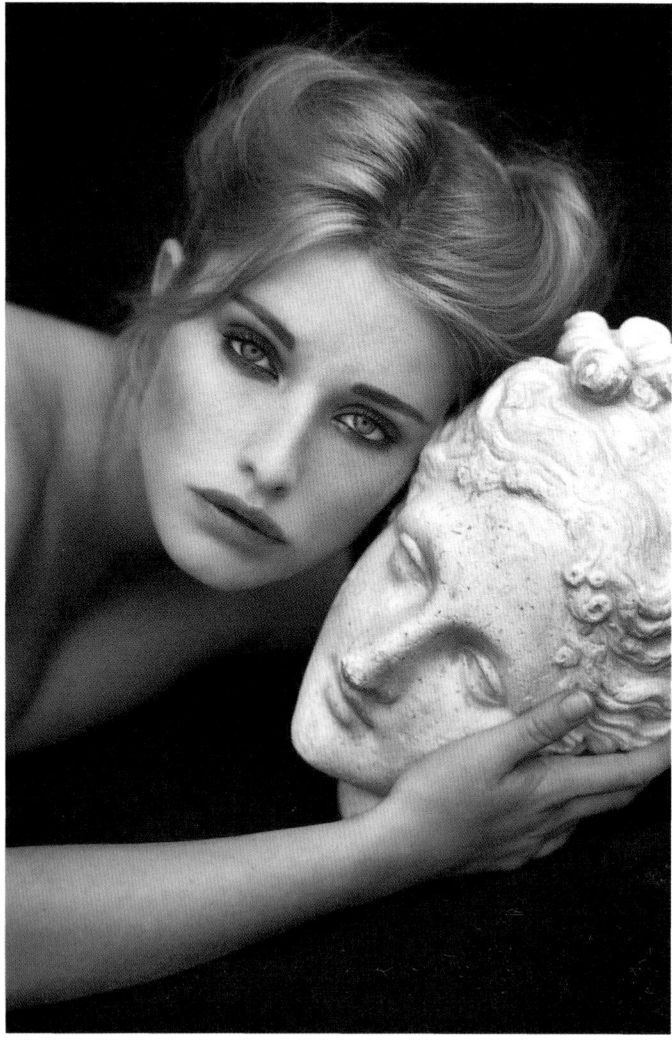

Marc Lagrange | *Alto Rilievo*, 2015

this one seems to engage directly with the ideas underlying the marriage we are
seeking to sanction. To begin with, unlike most of the other images where the models
are either dwarfed or overshadowed by the setting, here the two components — the
sculpture and the living head — are shown devoid of background and are of equal
size. The equilibrium gives rise to a placid tension born of parity, not, as in many
of the other images, a tension born of disparity such as large/small, clothed/naked,
figure/relief and so on. More importantly, when coupled in a single image, each
element is enriched, successfully complementing the other and creating thereby a
whole transcending the sum of its constituent parts. This living woman's face and her
expression are sculptural: classic, ideal, poised; attractive, yet aloof and inaccessible.
On the other hand, the juxtaposition transforms the sculpture's blank eyes, stifled
mouth and apparent coldness. Guided by her caressing hand, it is filled by Henrard's
brimming carnality, by the unblinking stare of her impeccably painted eyes and by
the lushness of her lips. In short, the flower becomes sculptural, and the sculpture,
in turn, becomes floral.'

And now, raise high the curtain, stage hands, like Ares and Aphrodite in their stride,
bring in the nuptial pair.

Puṣpa

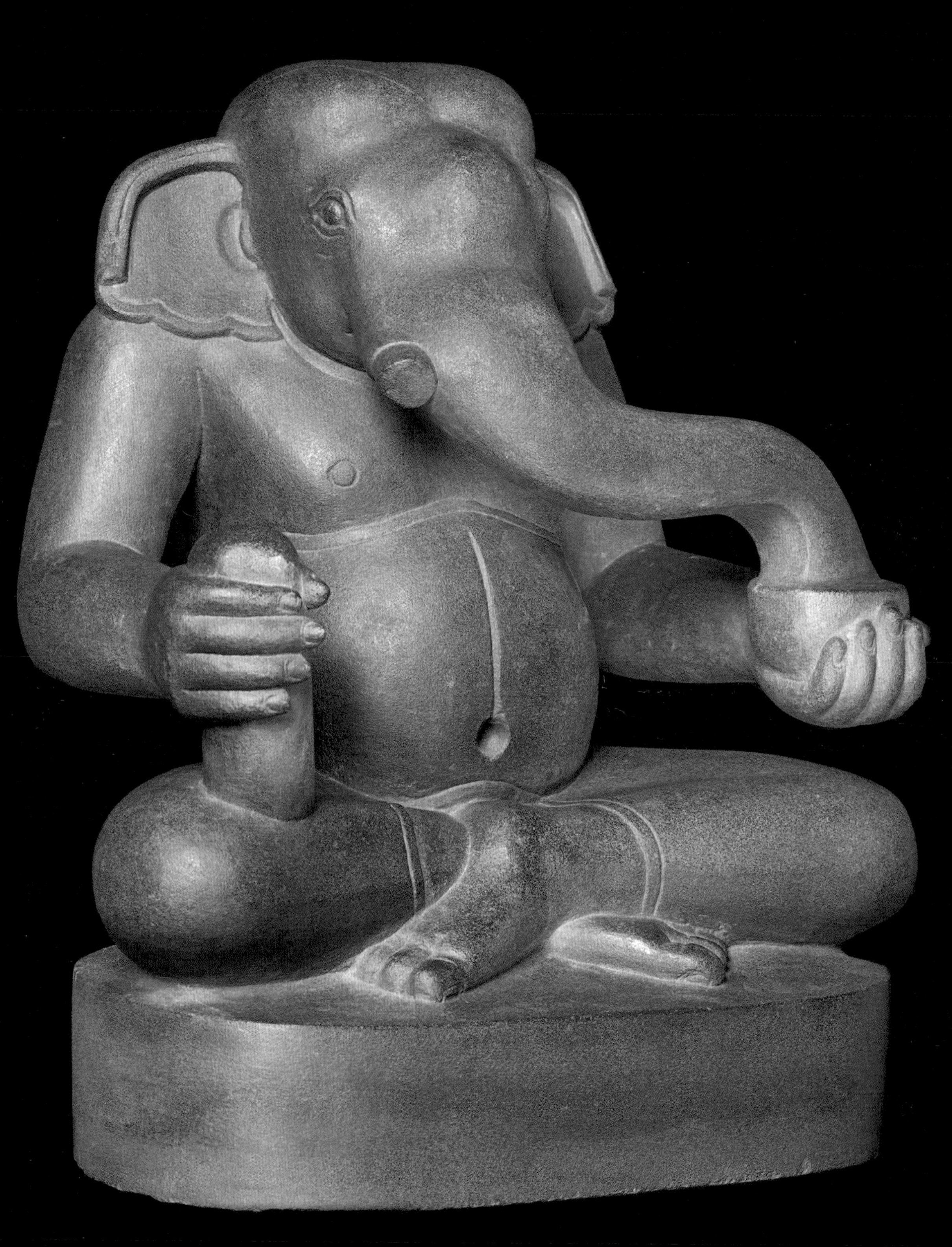

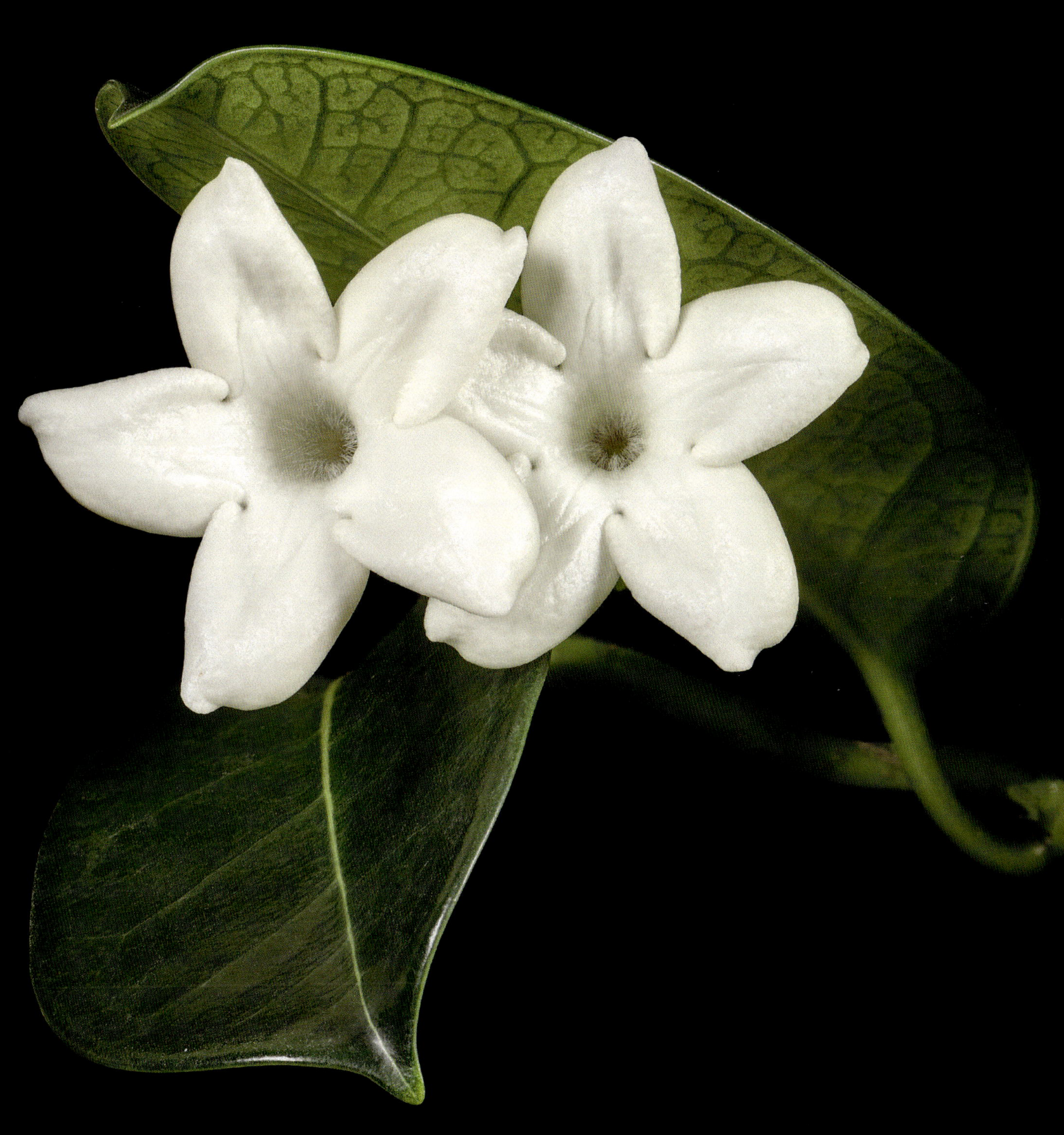

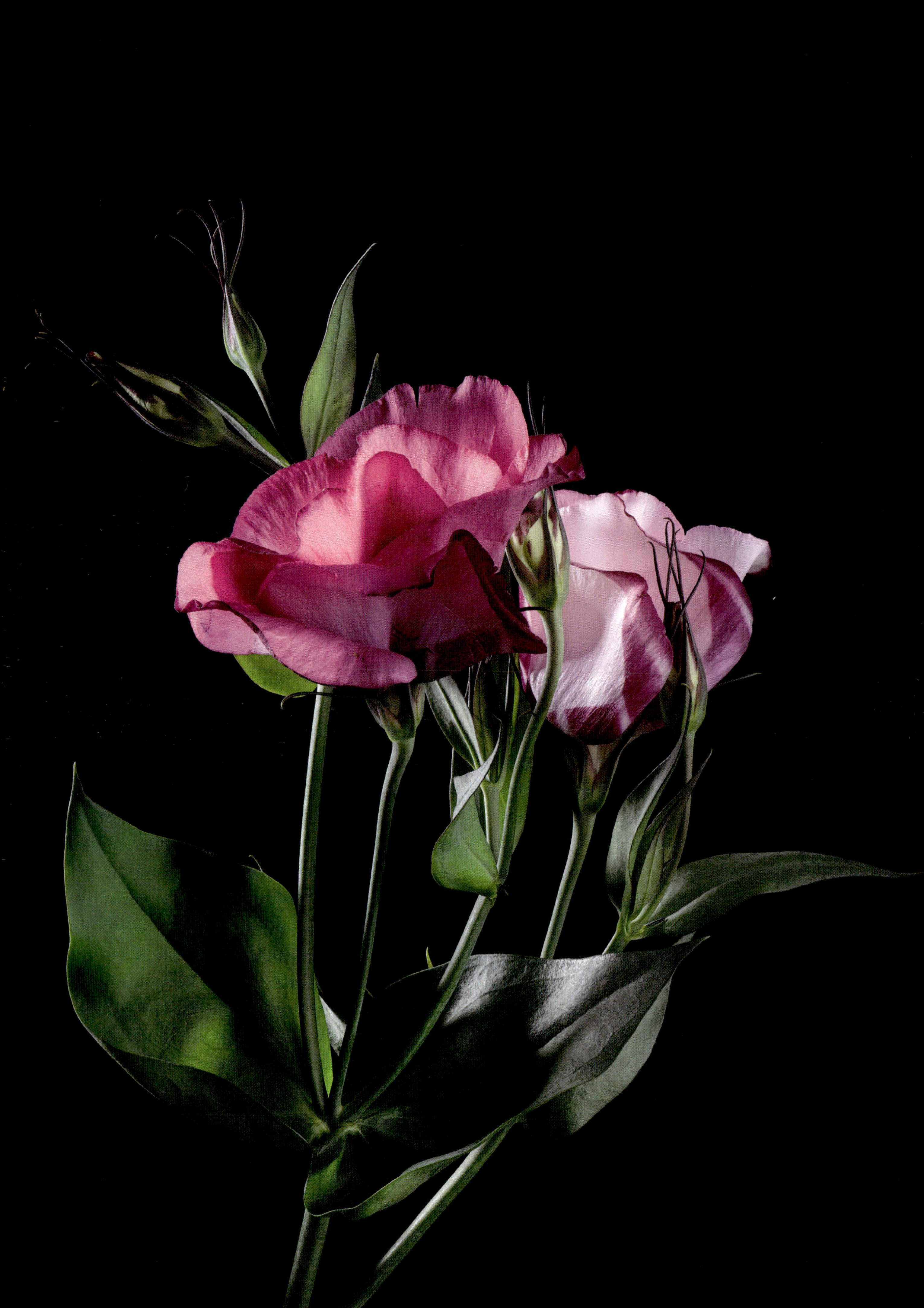

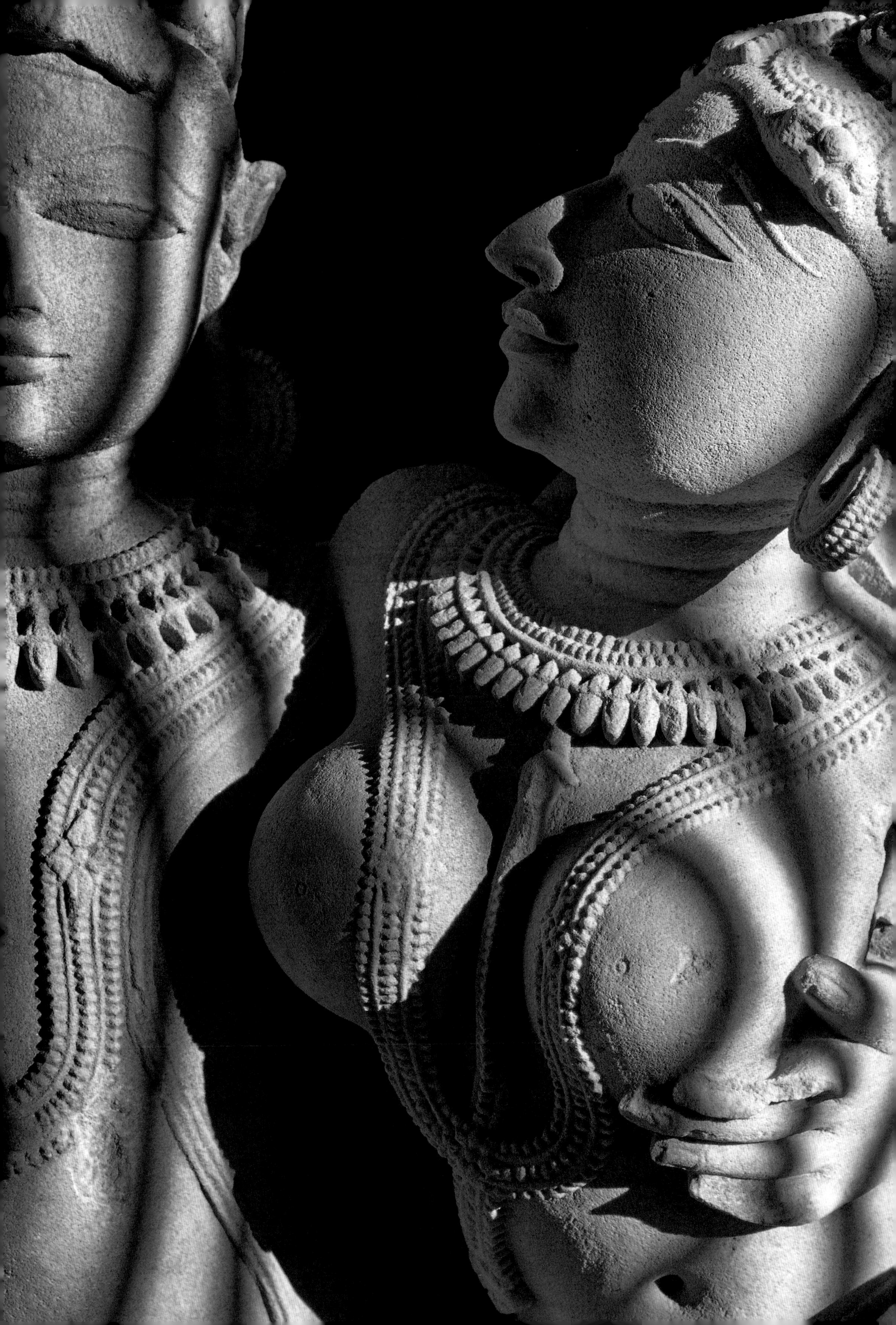

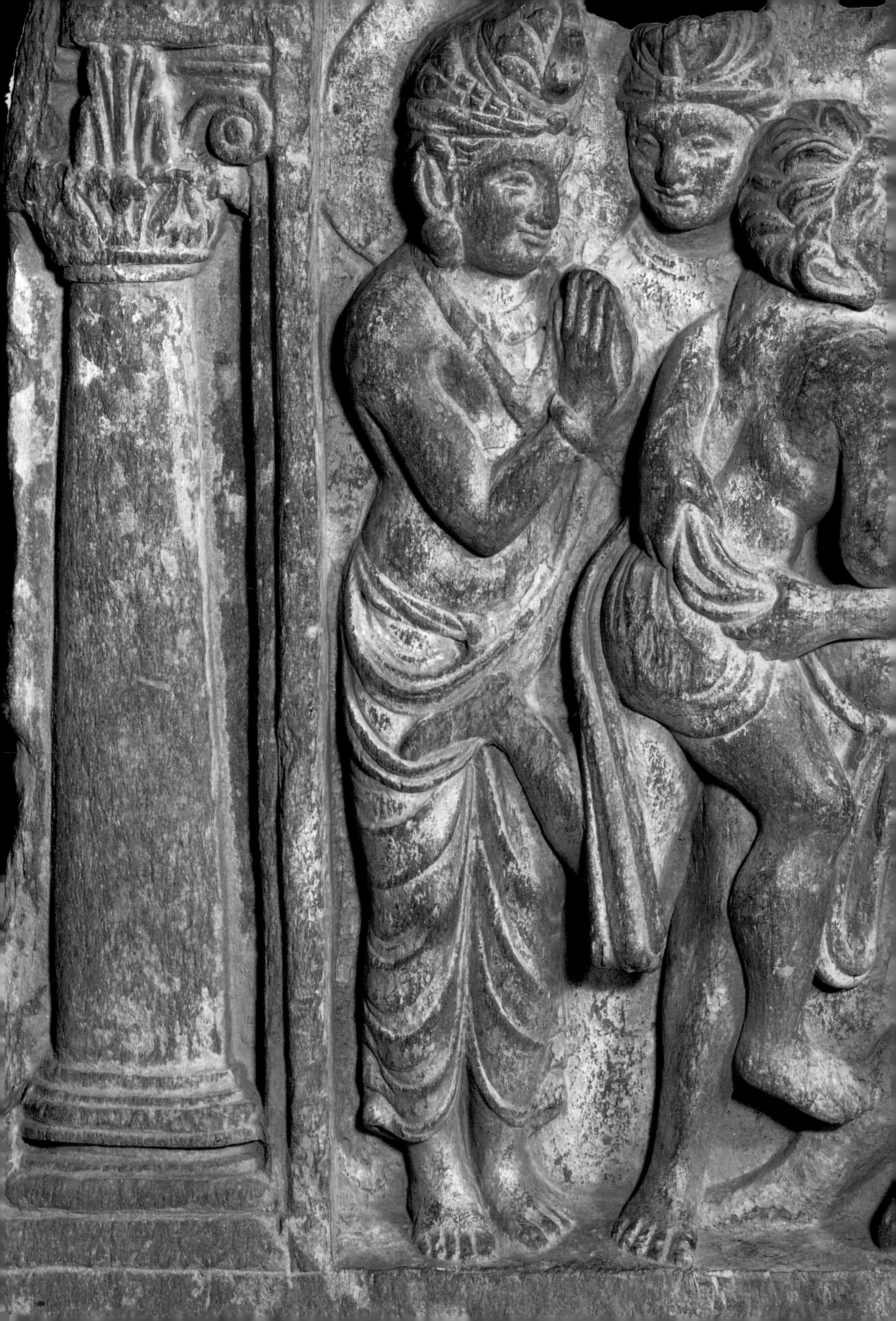

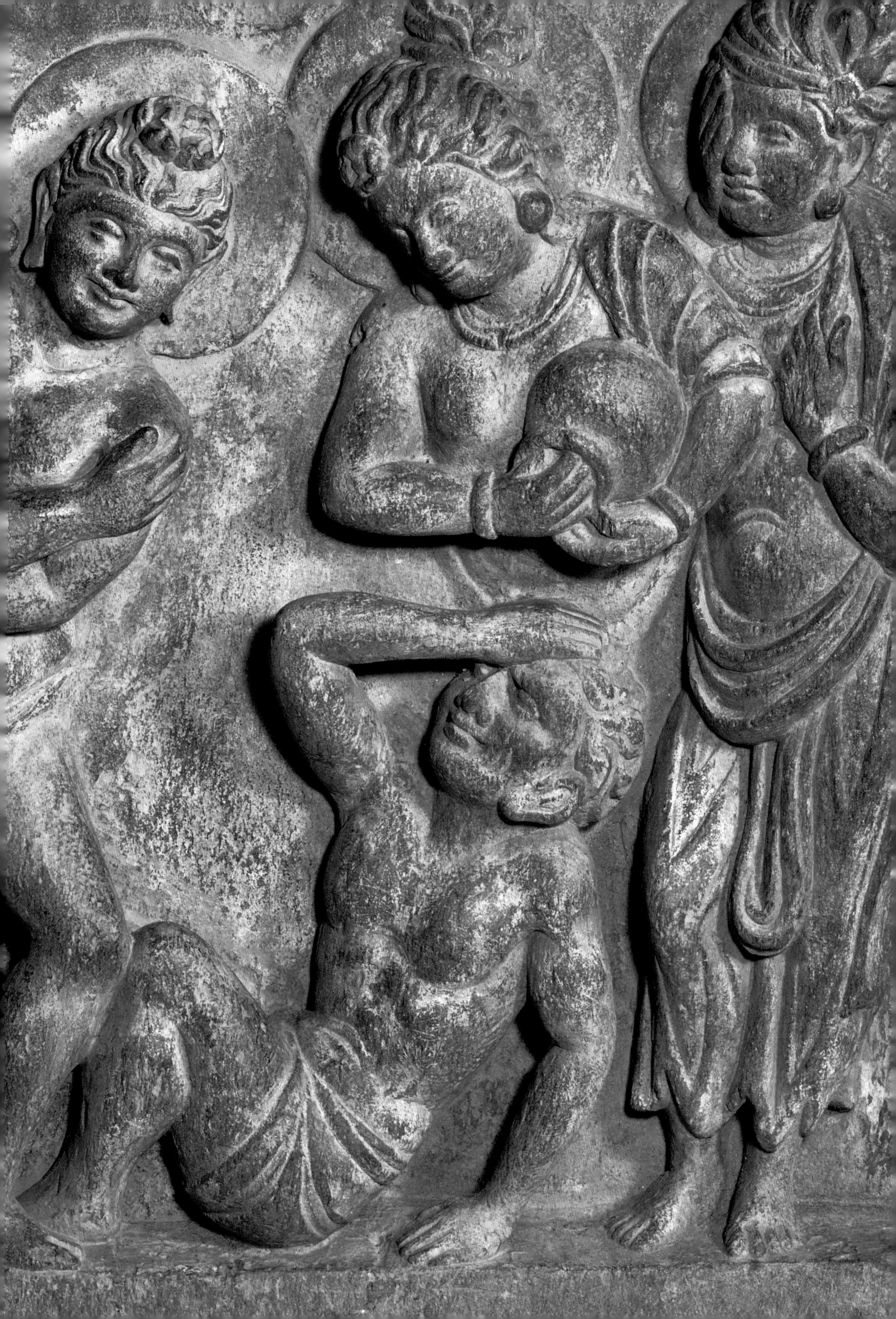

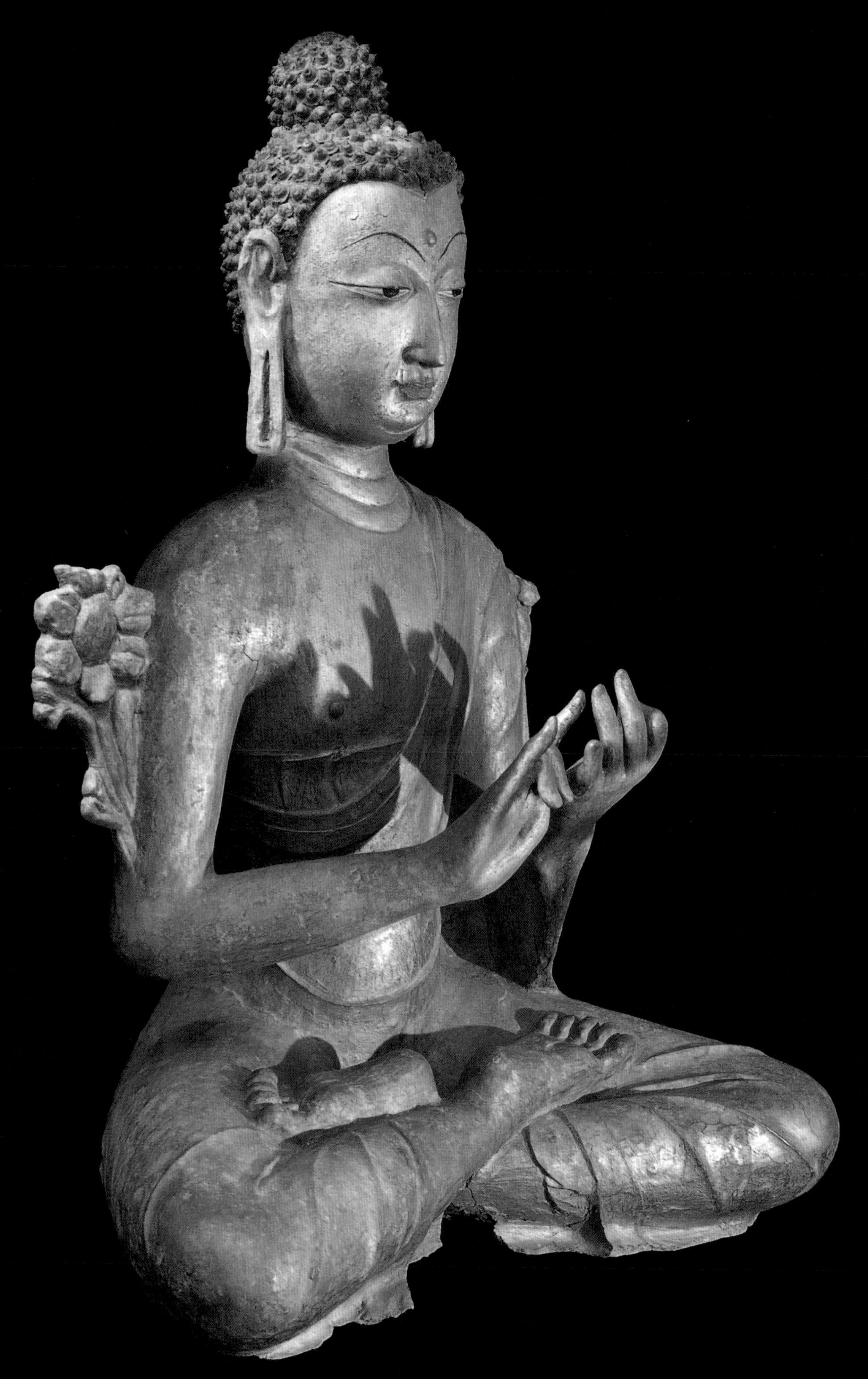

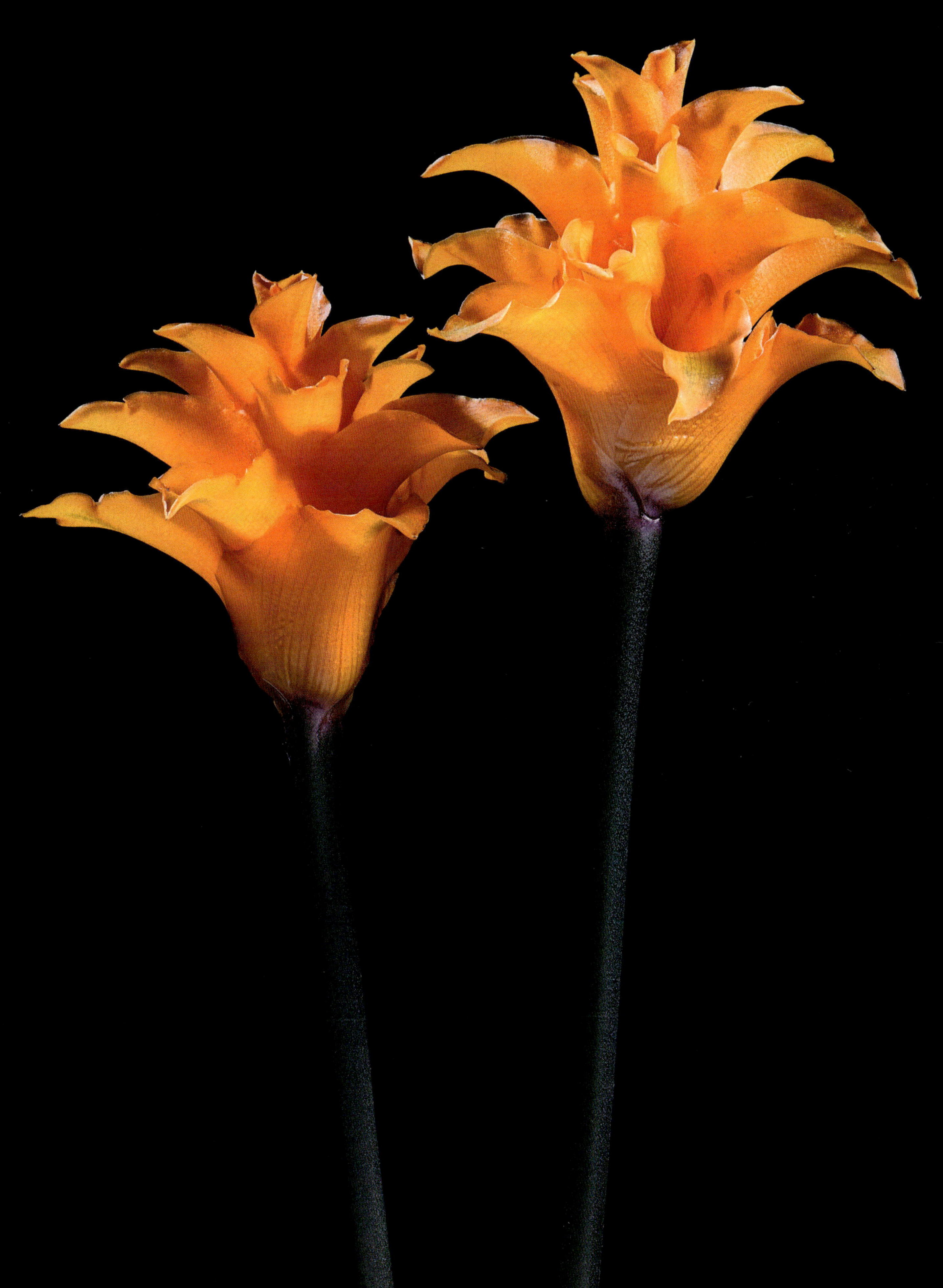

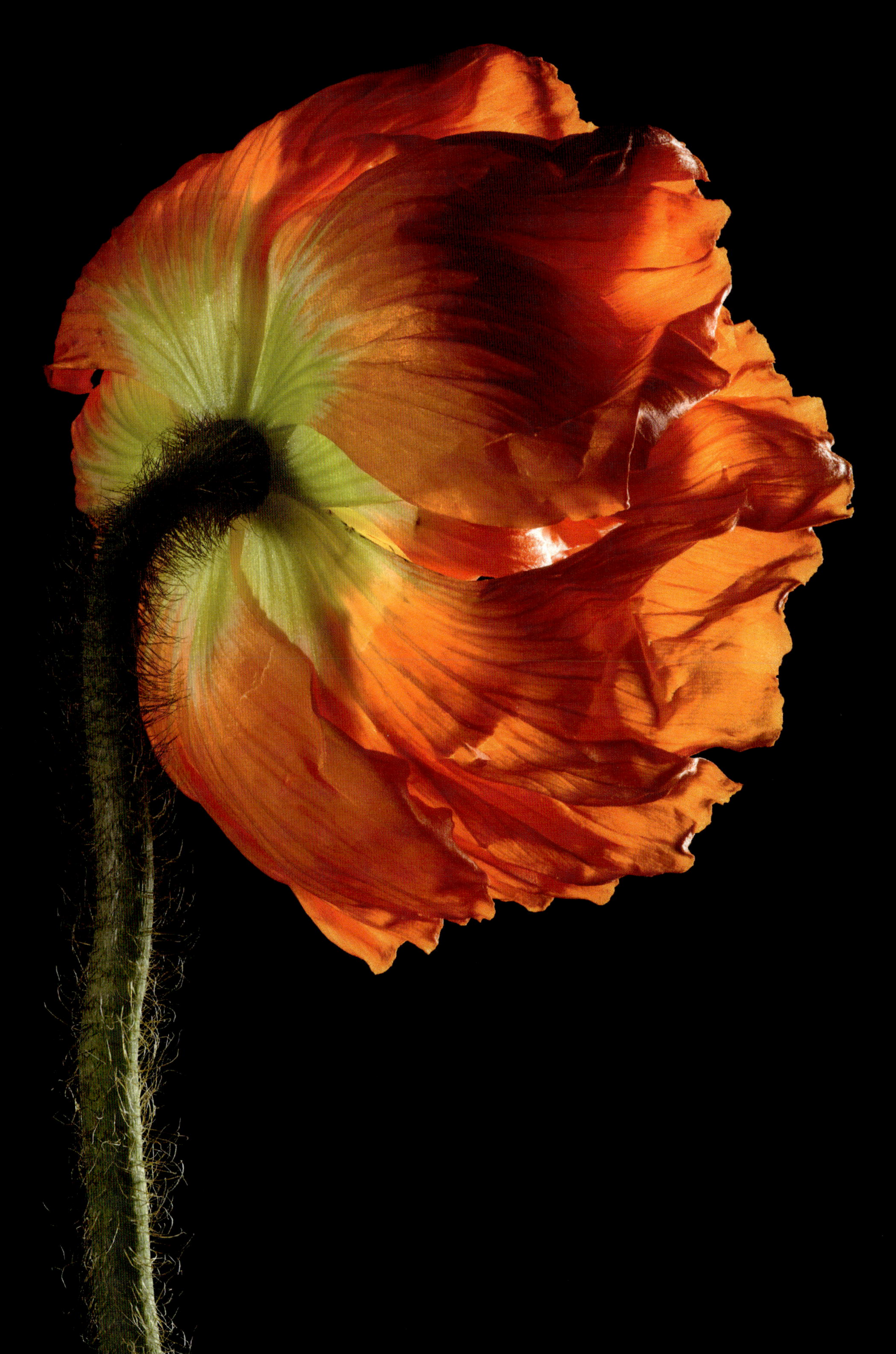

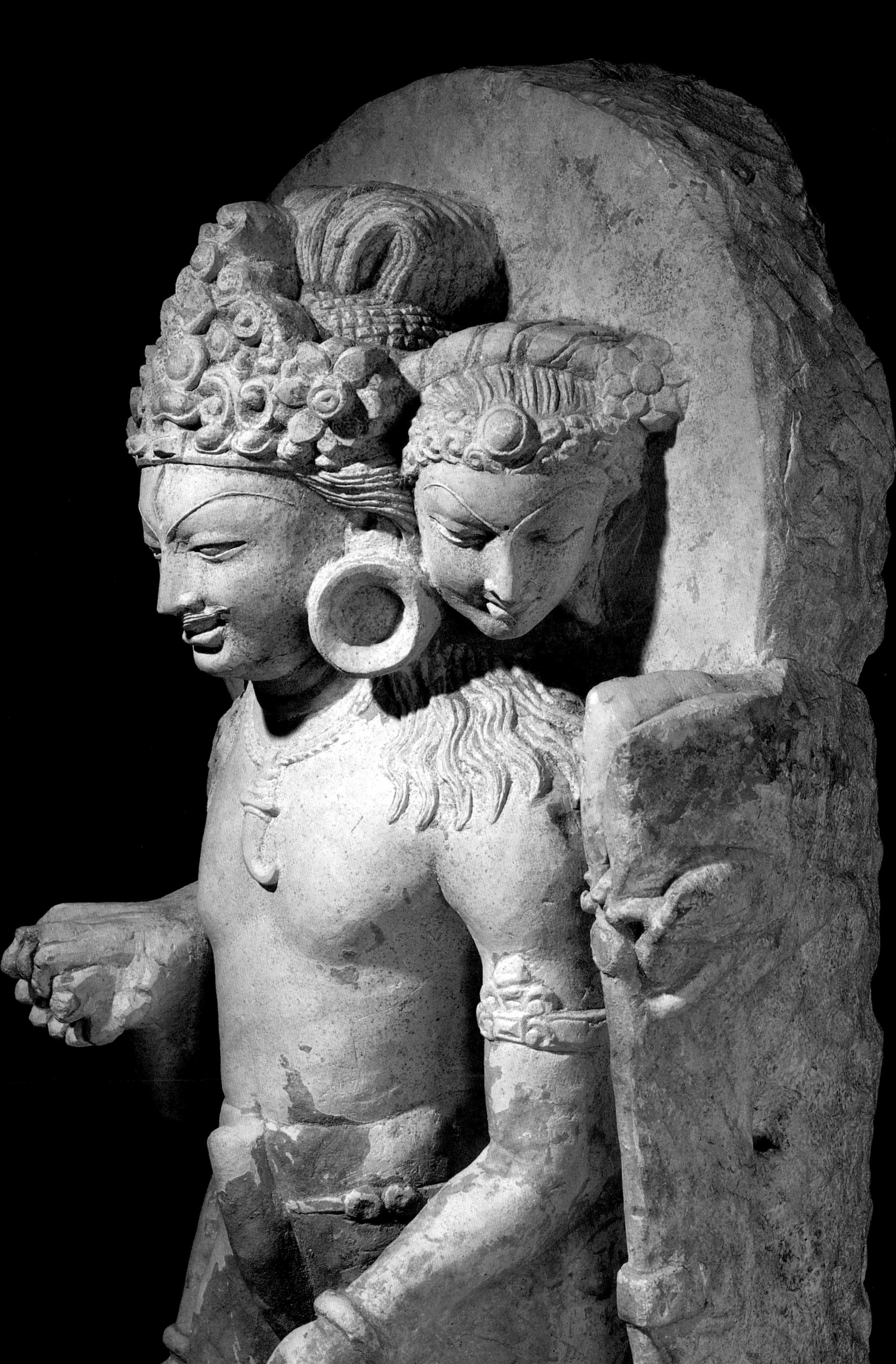

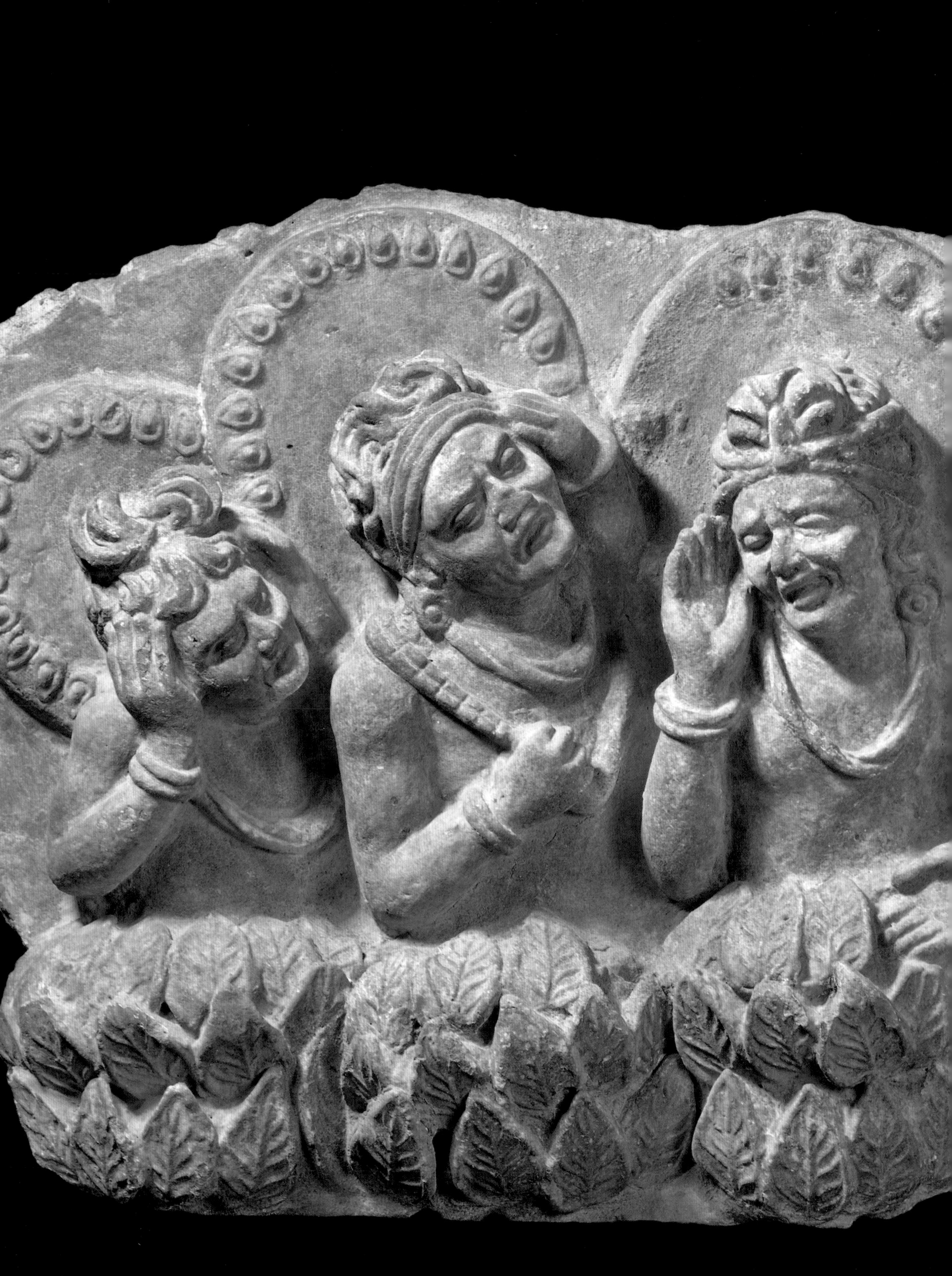

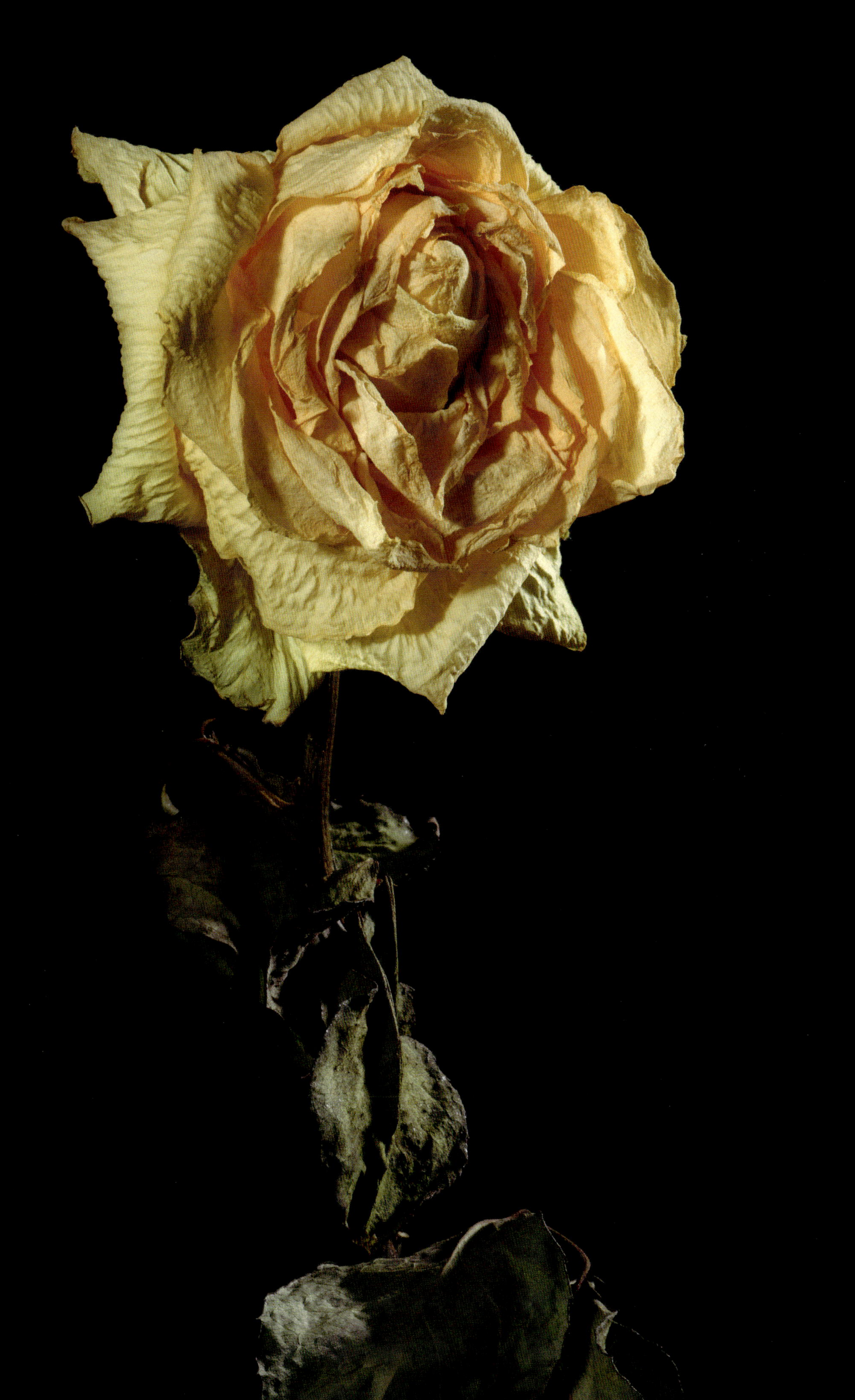

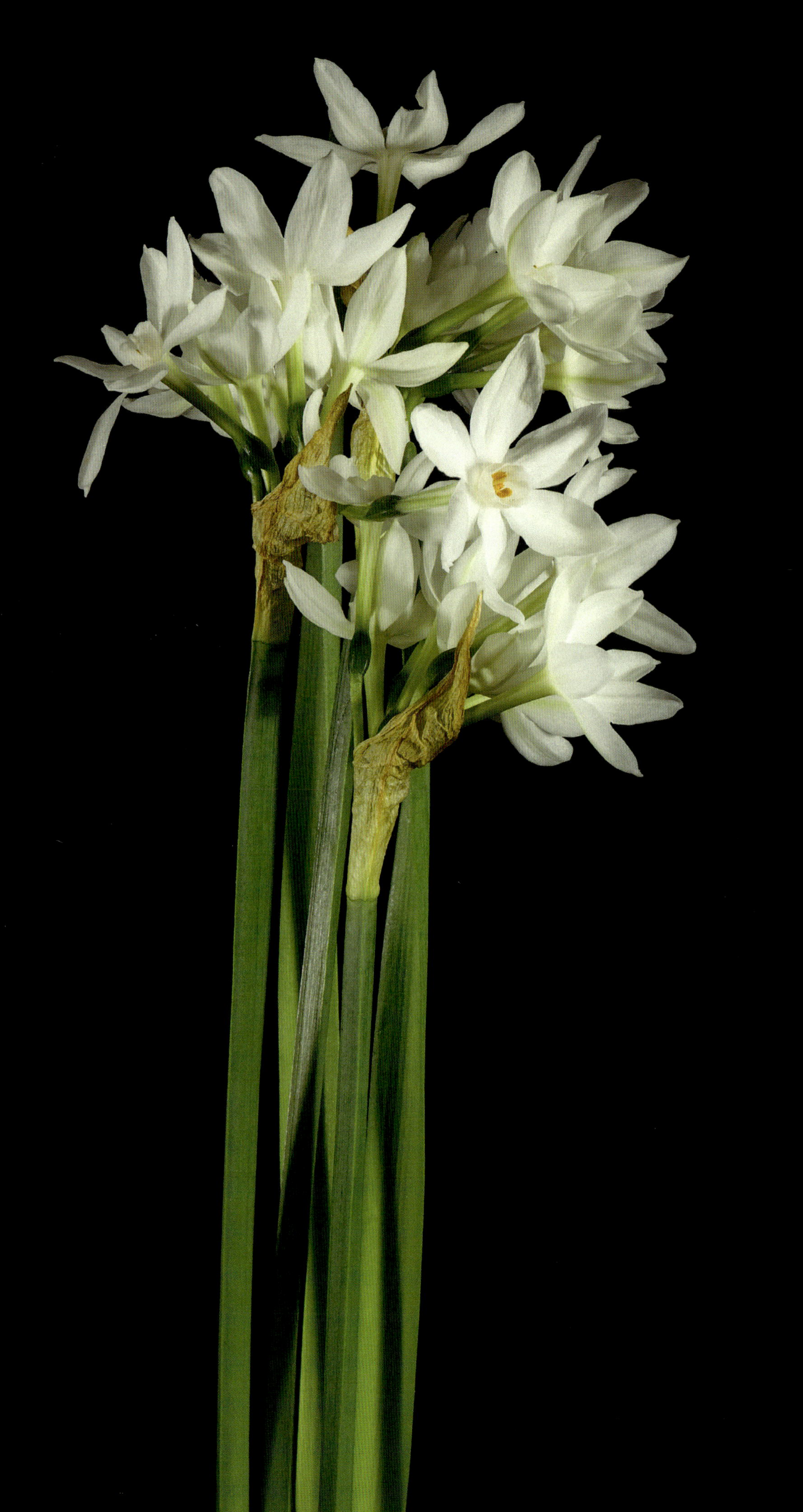

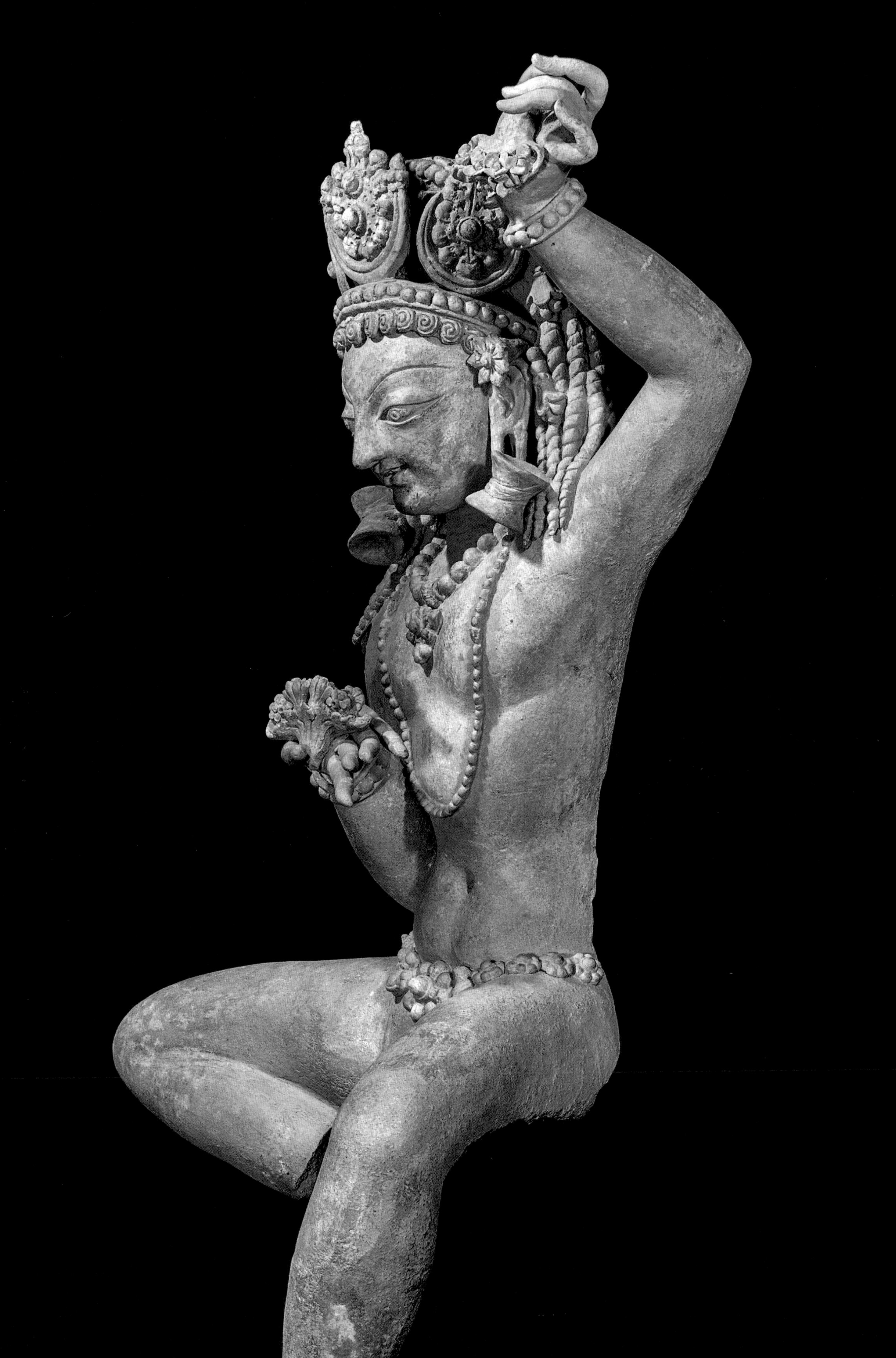

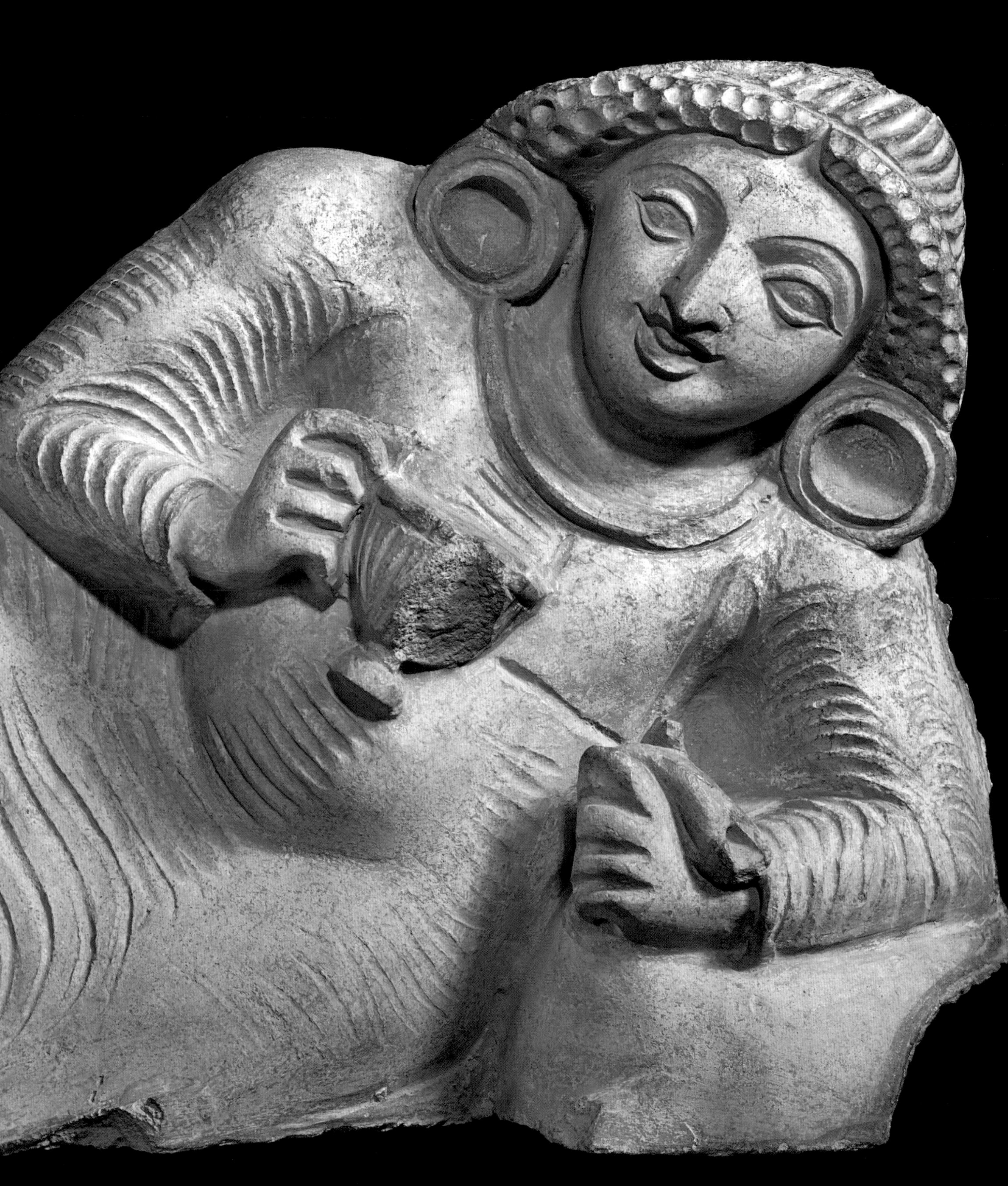

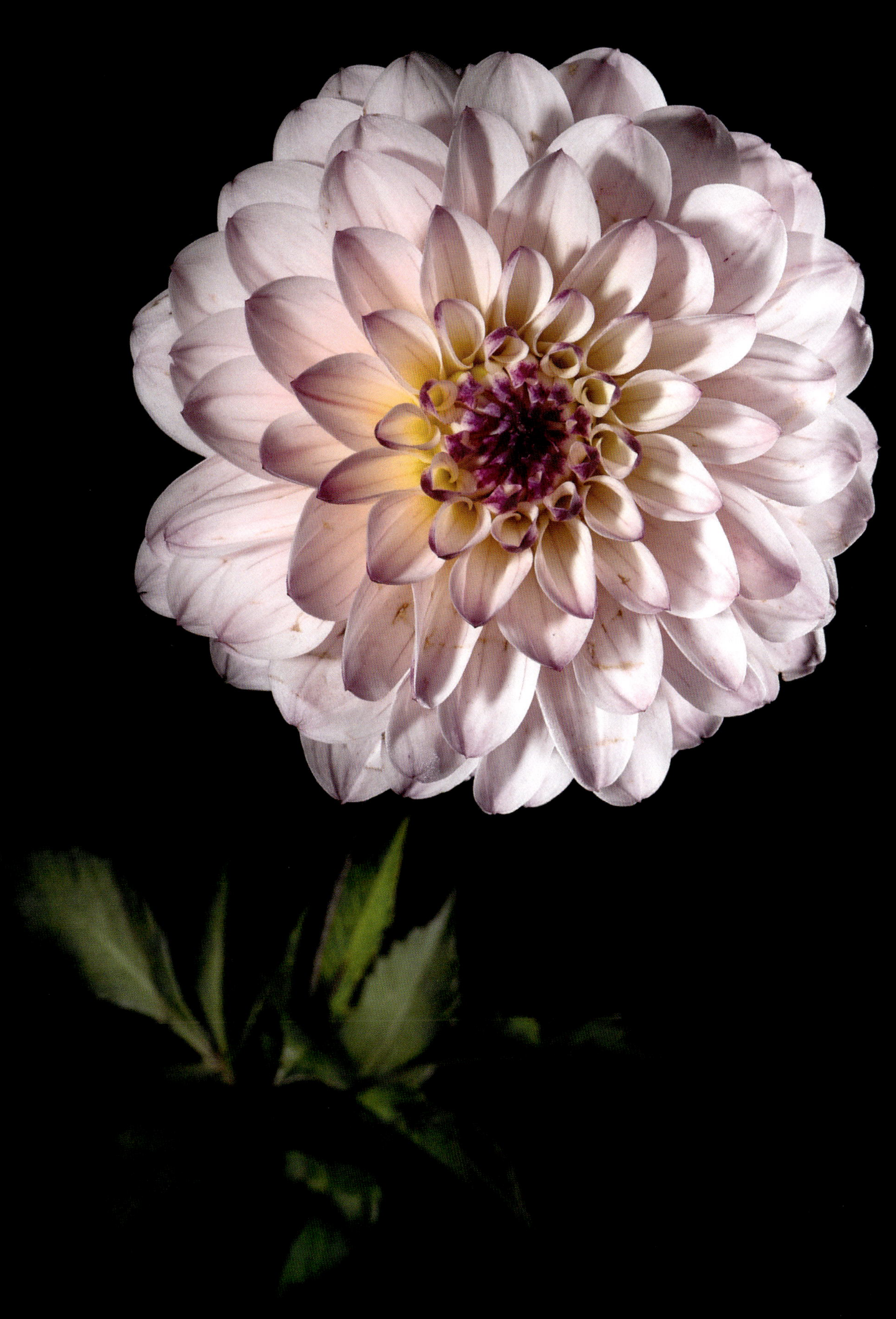

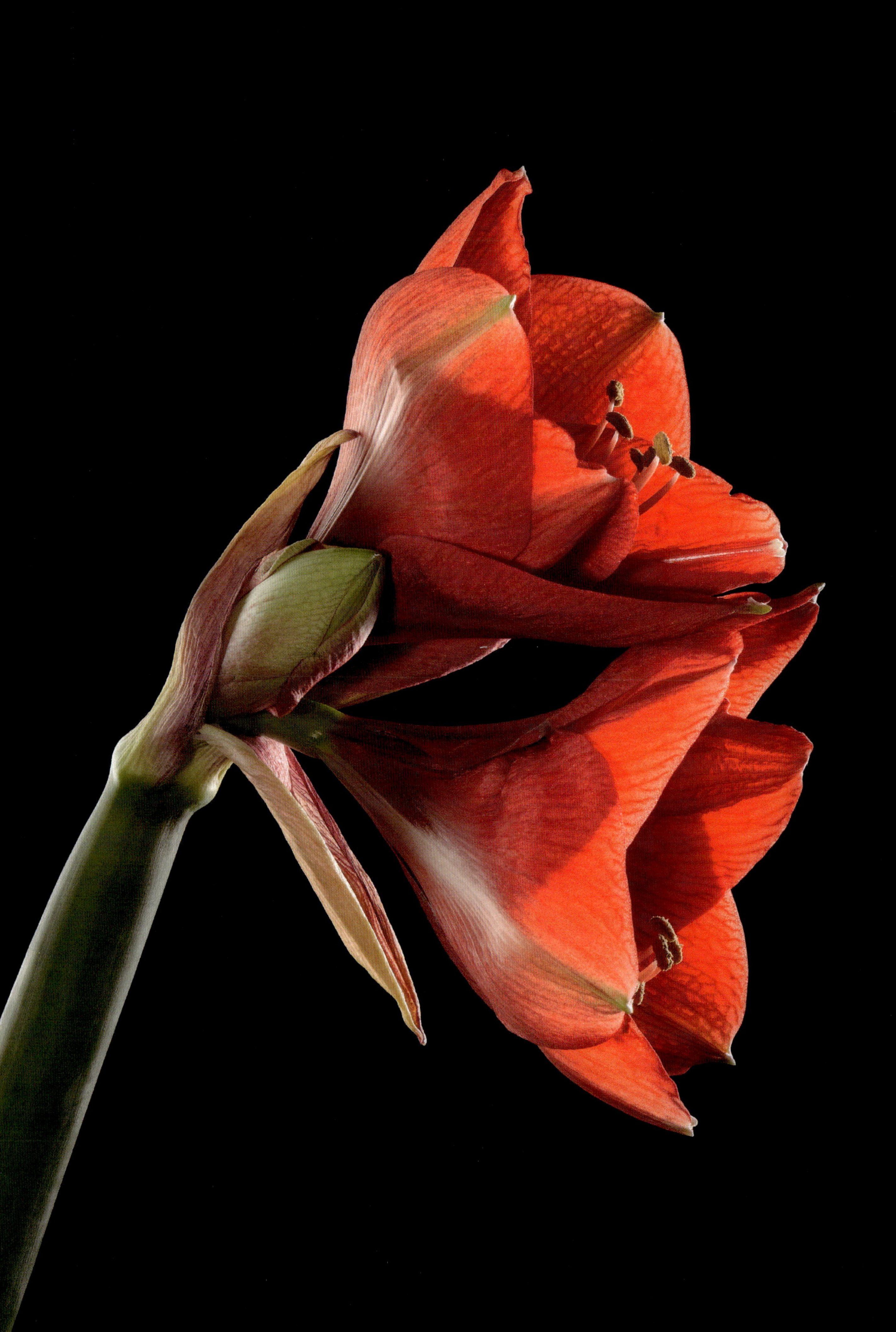

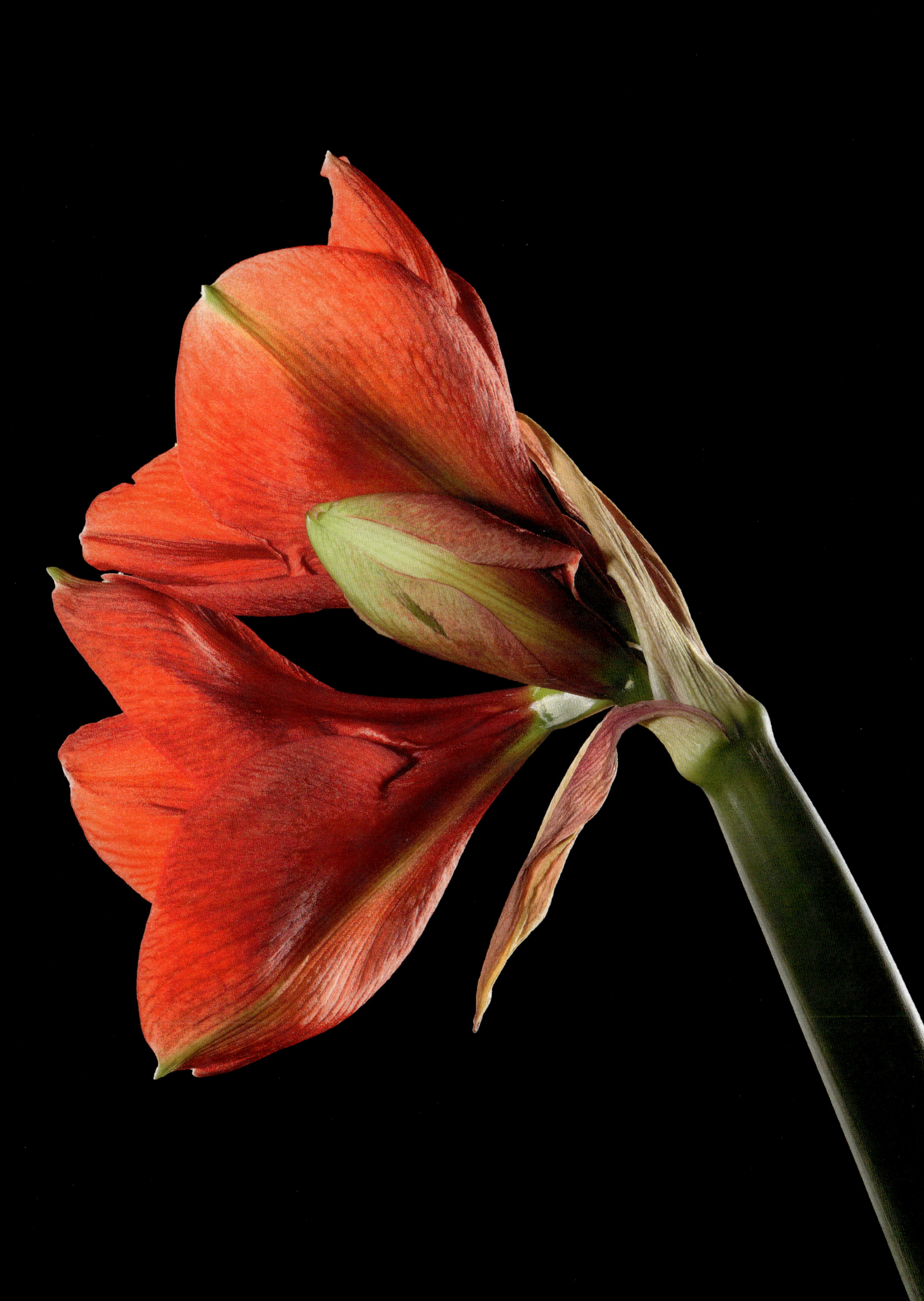

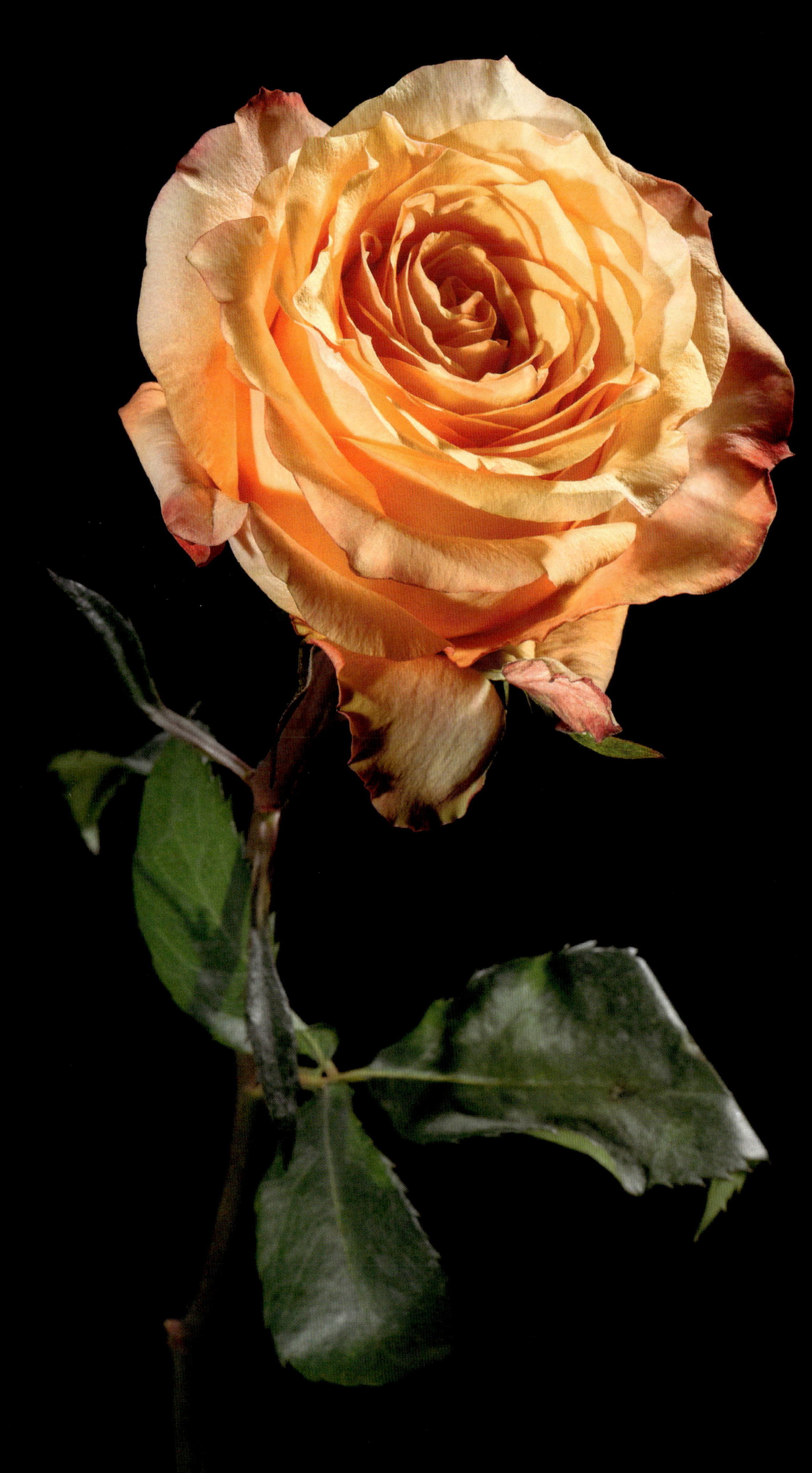

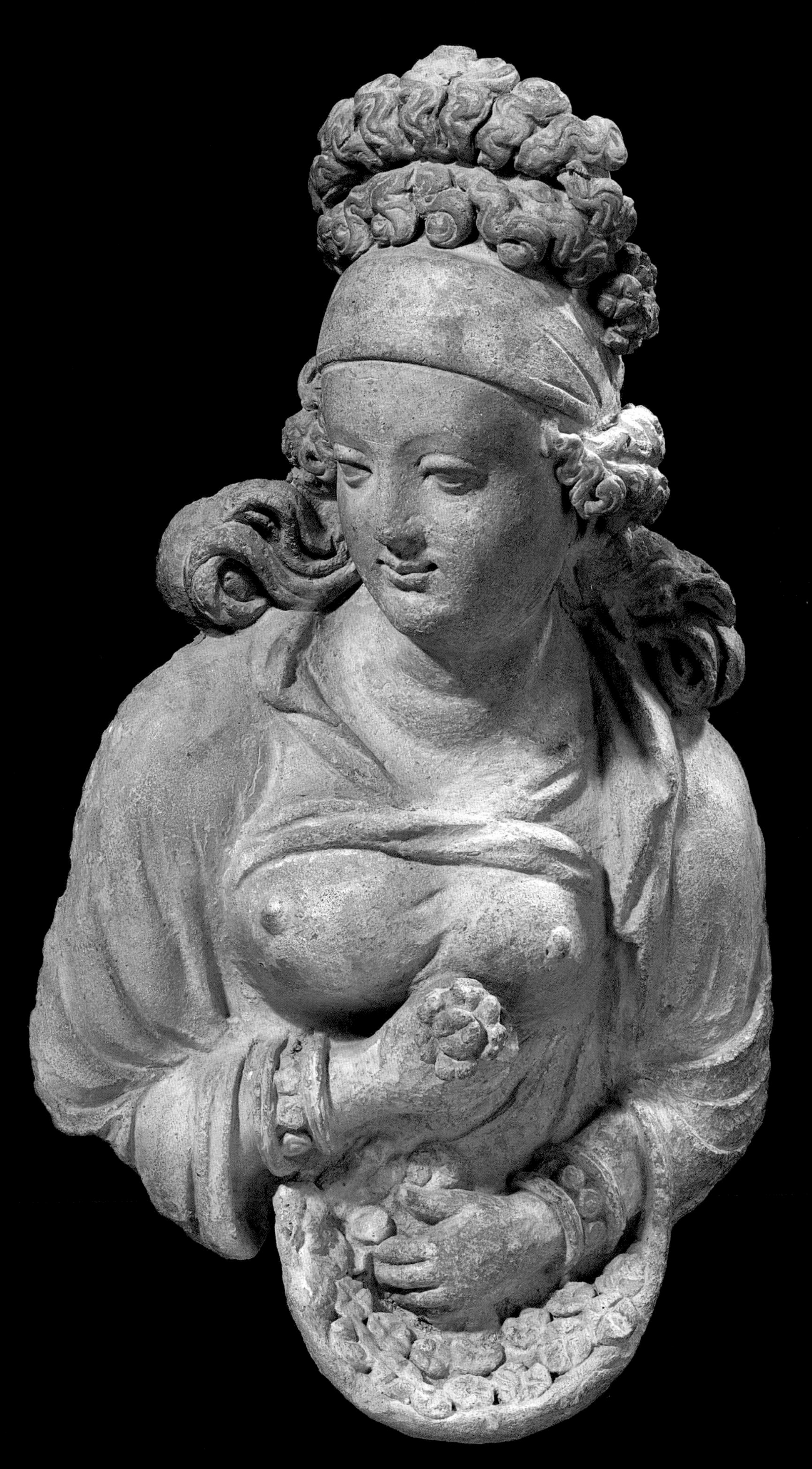

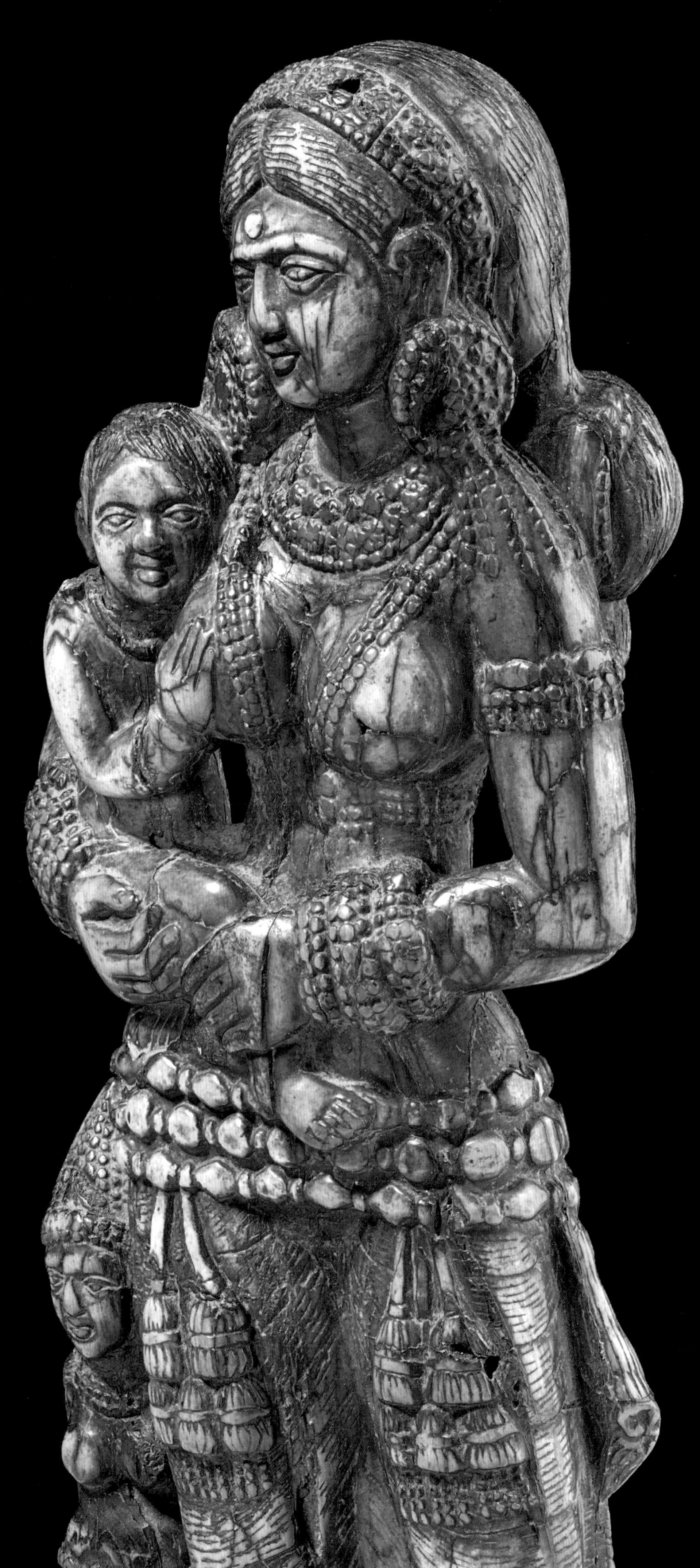

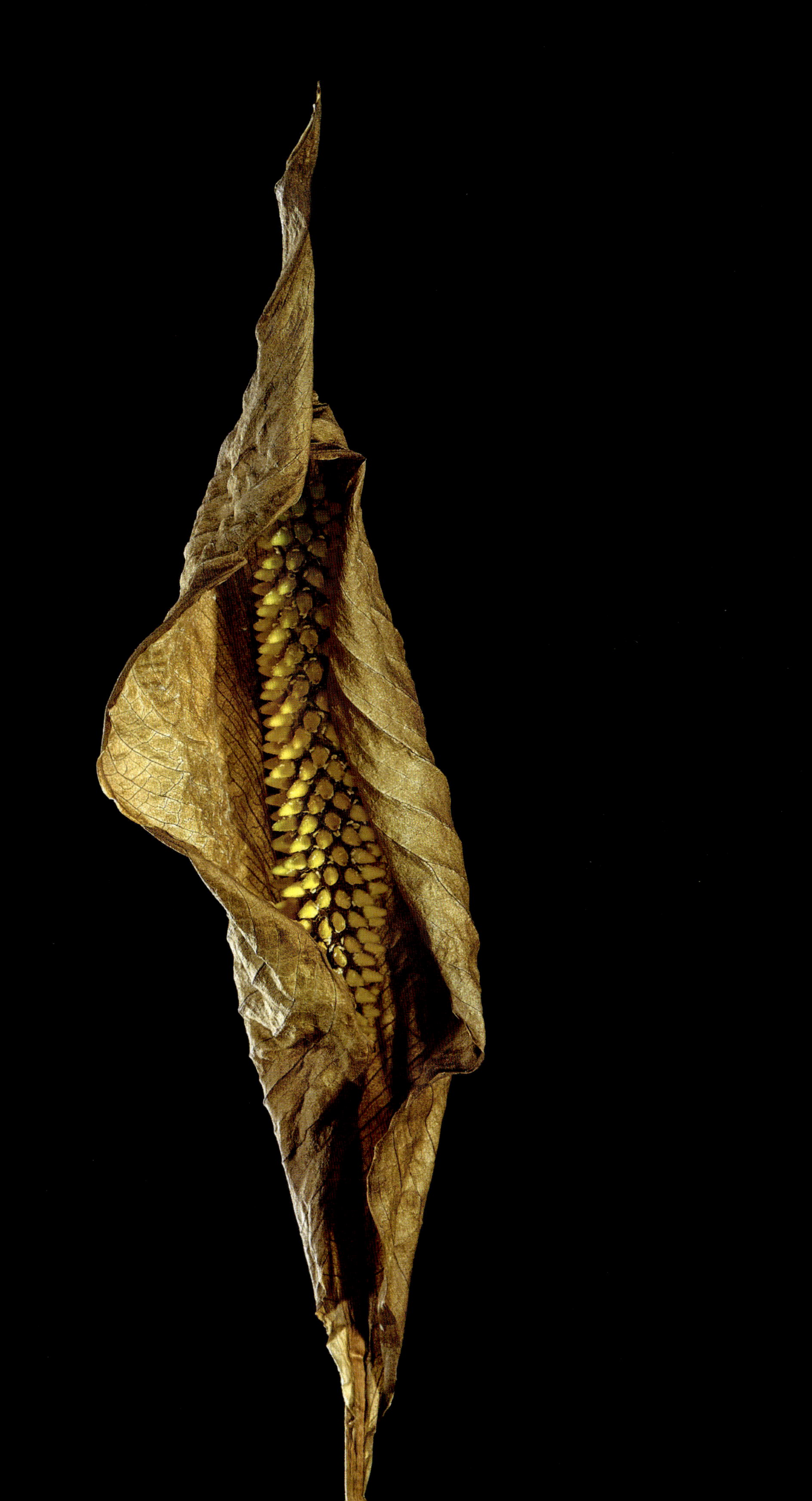

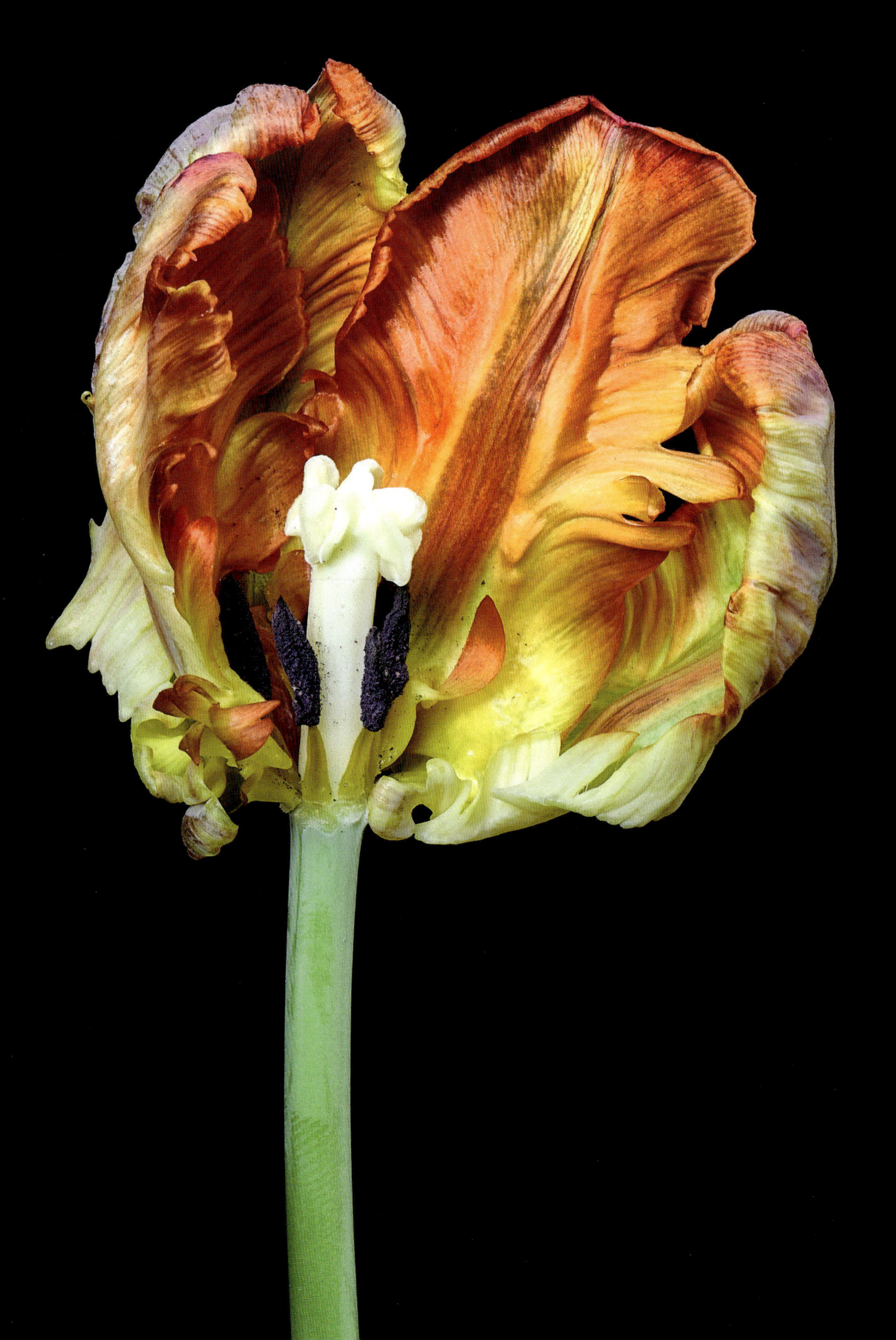

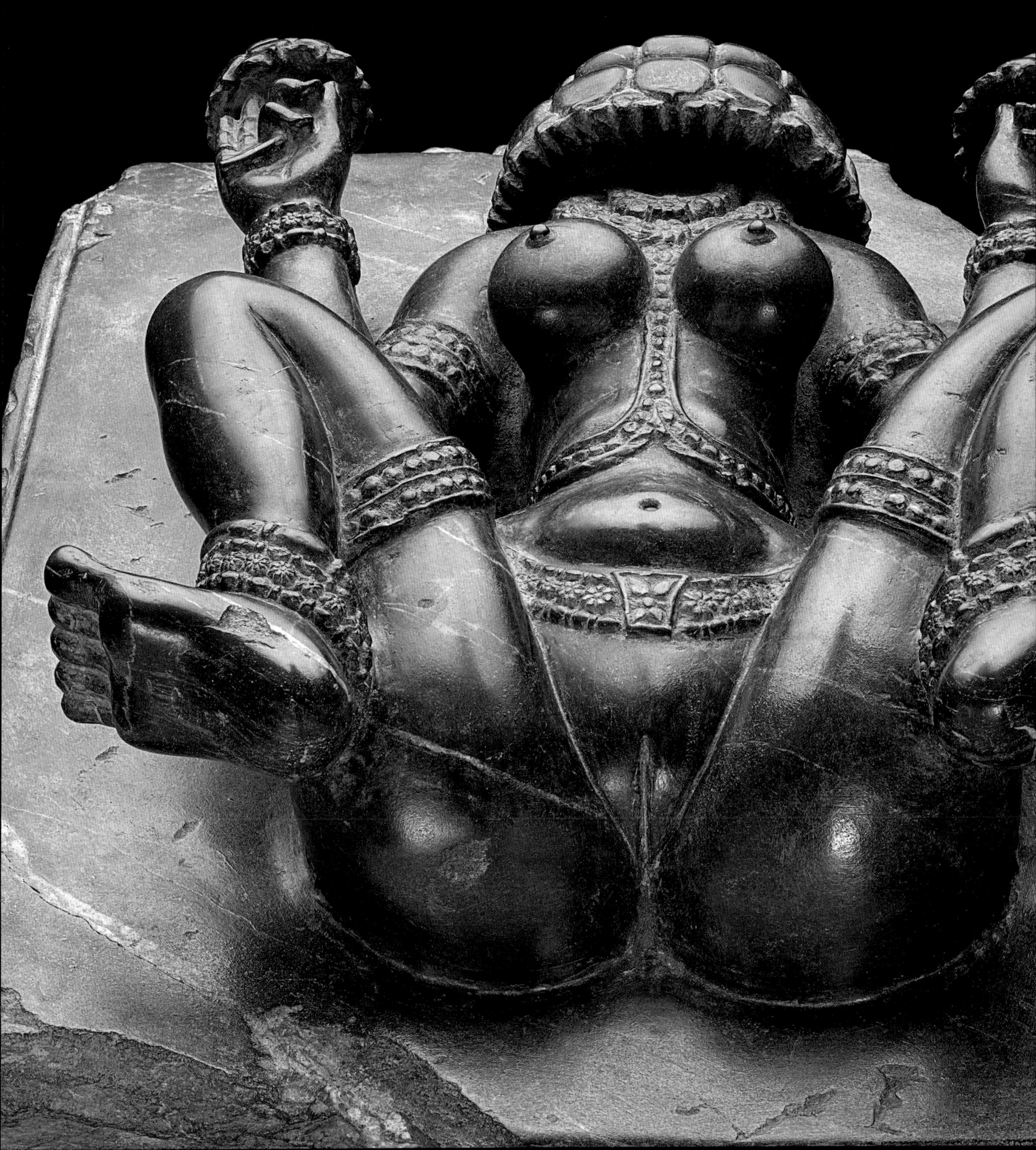

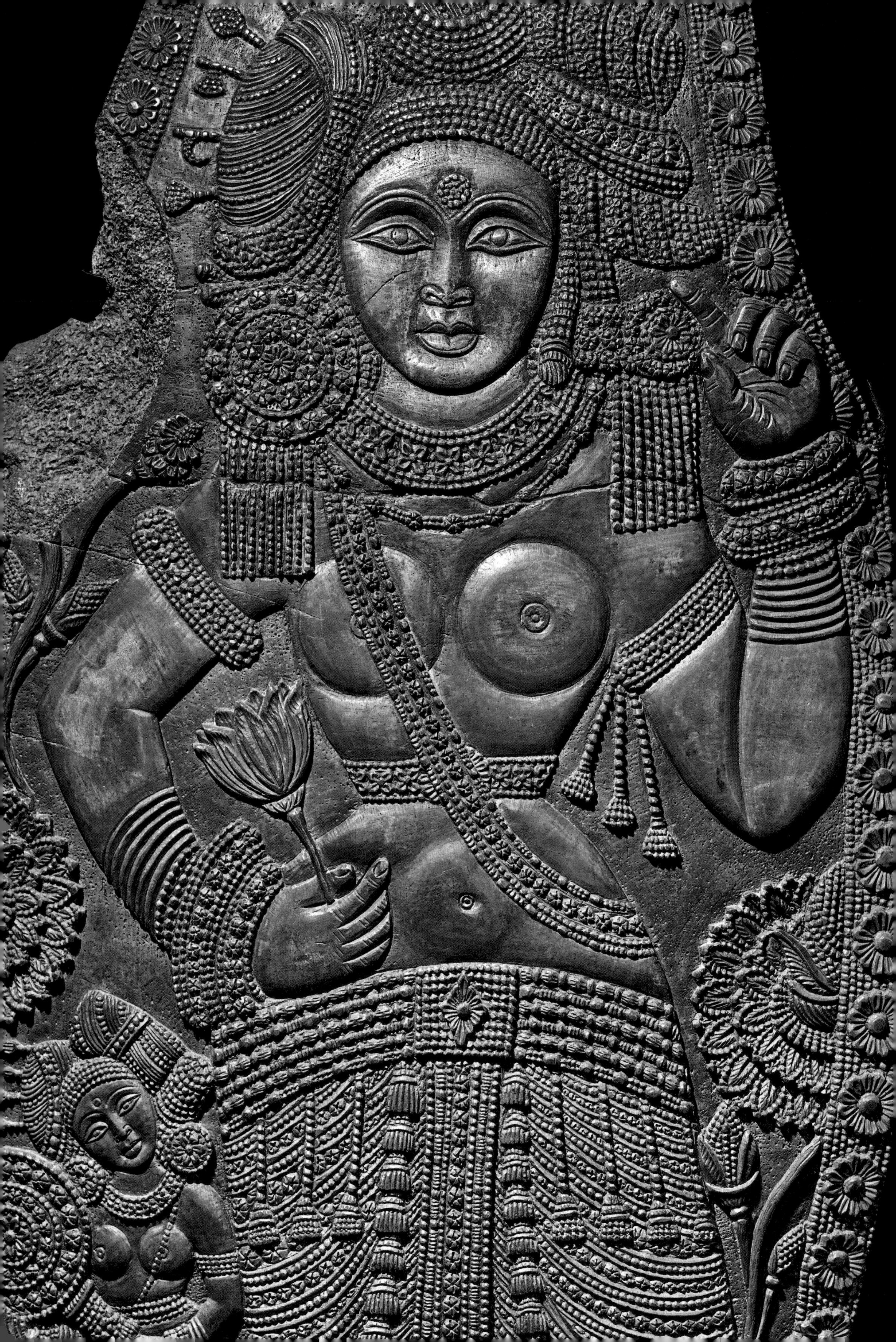

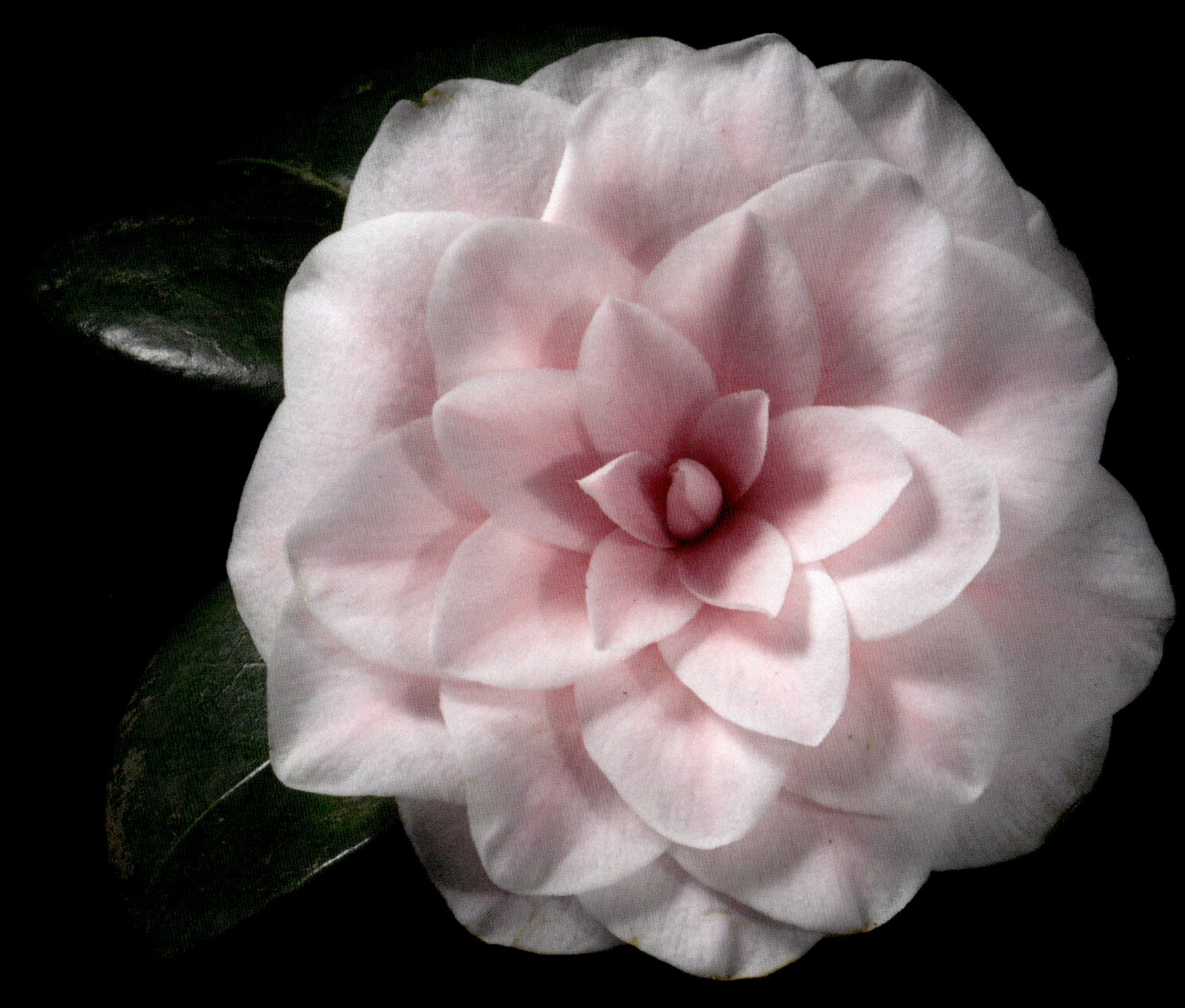

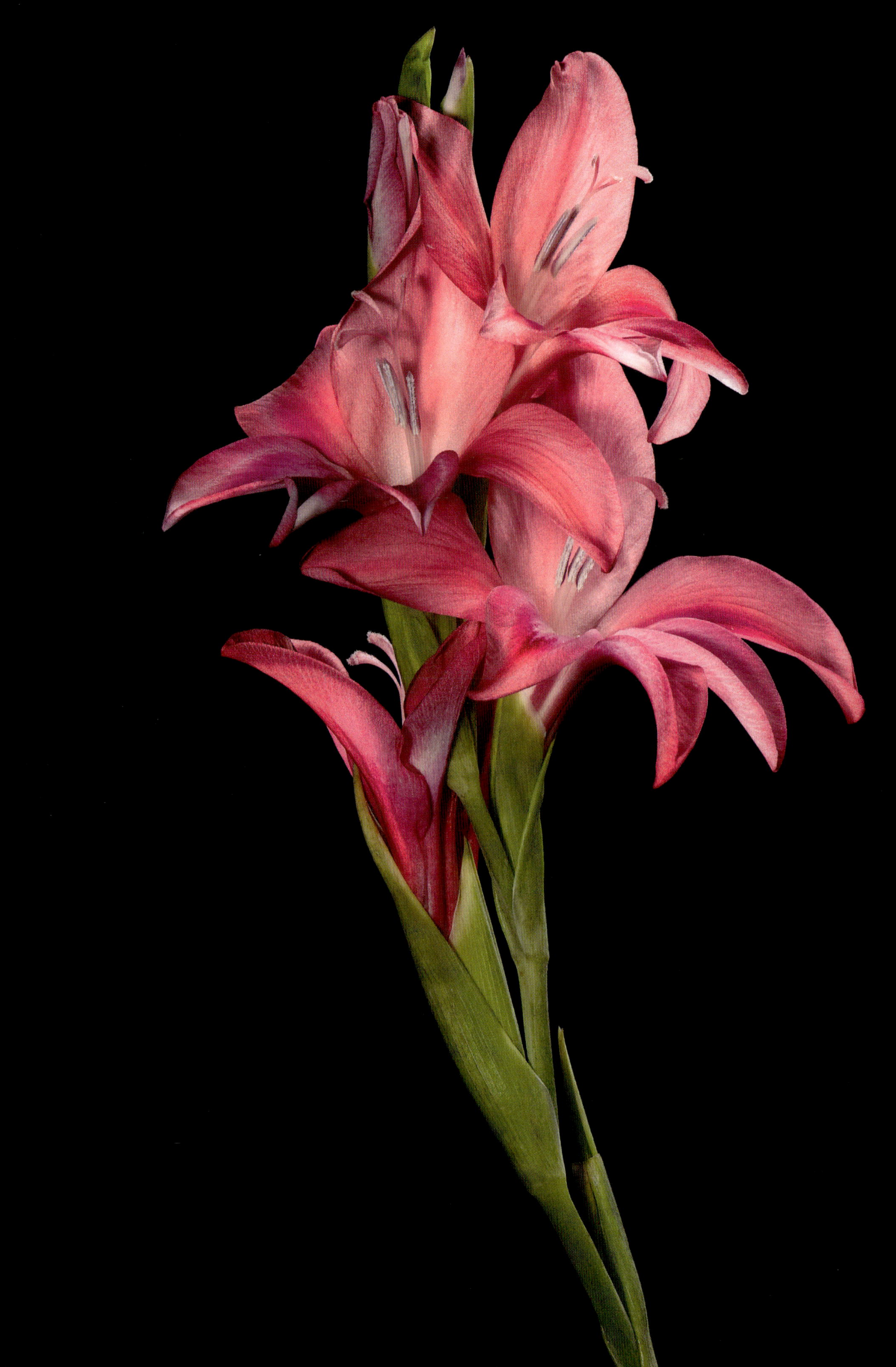

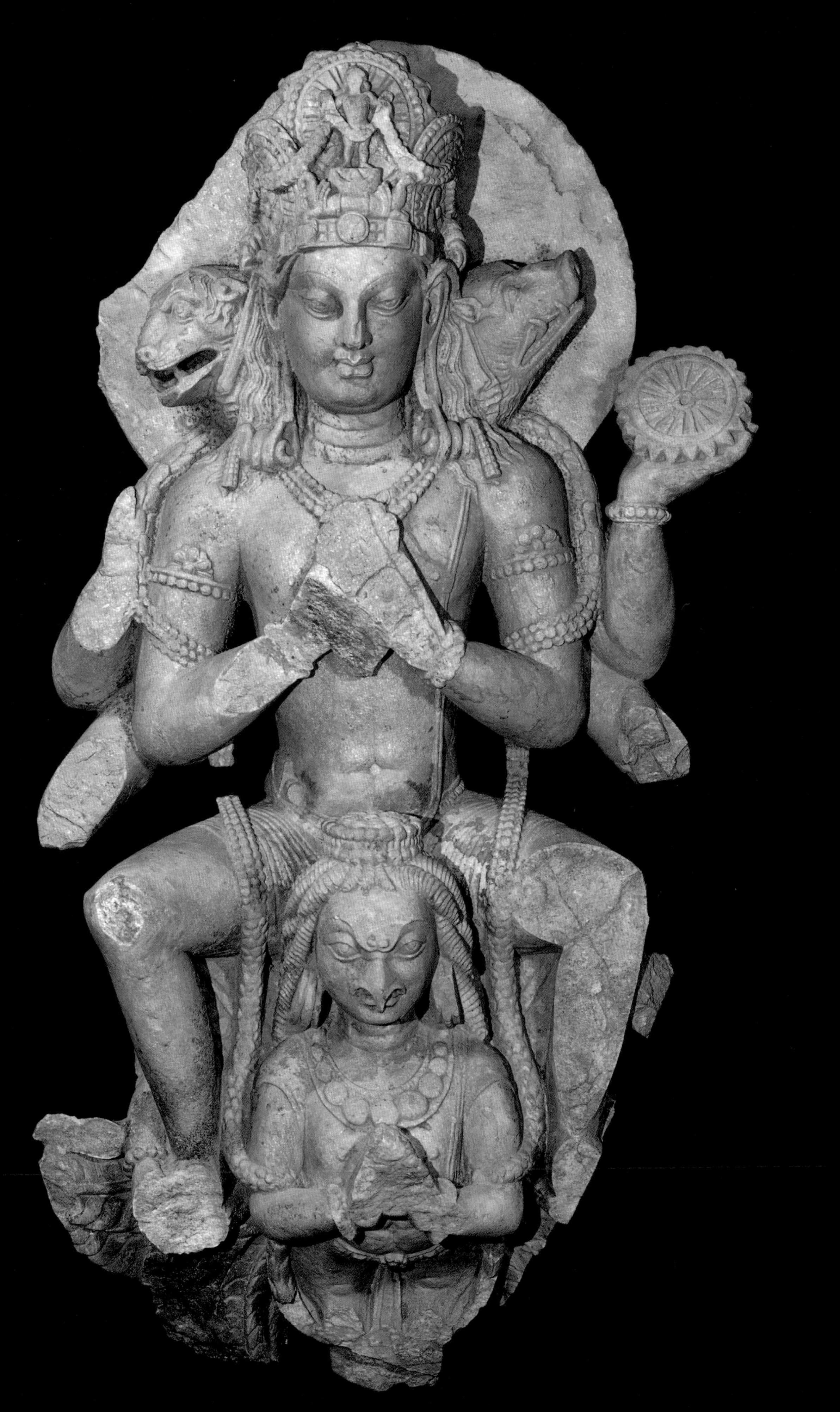

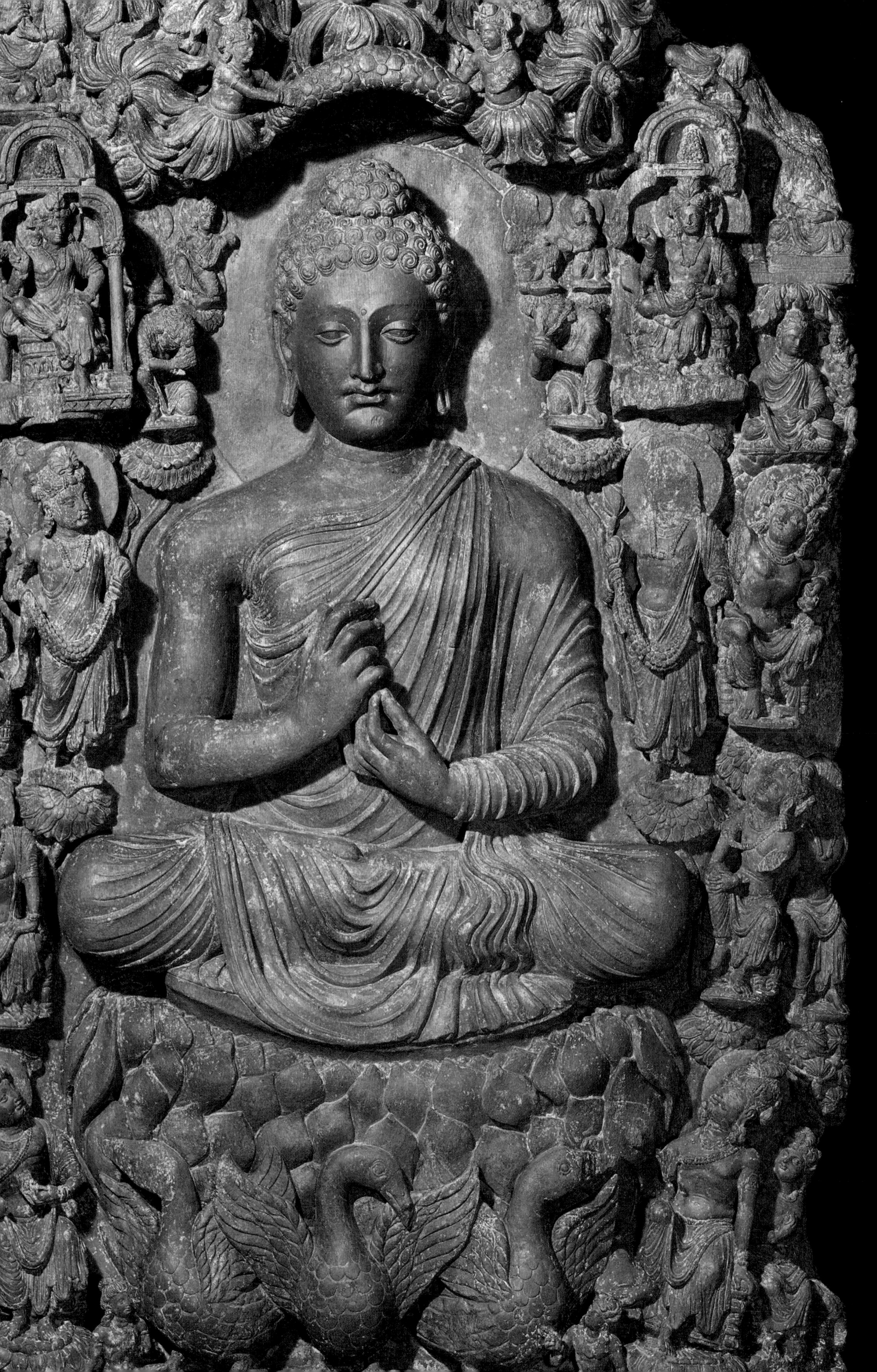

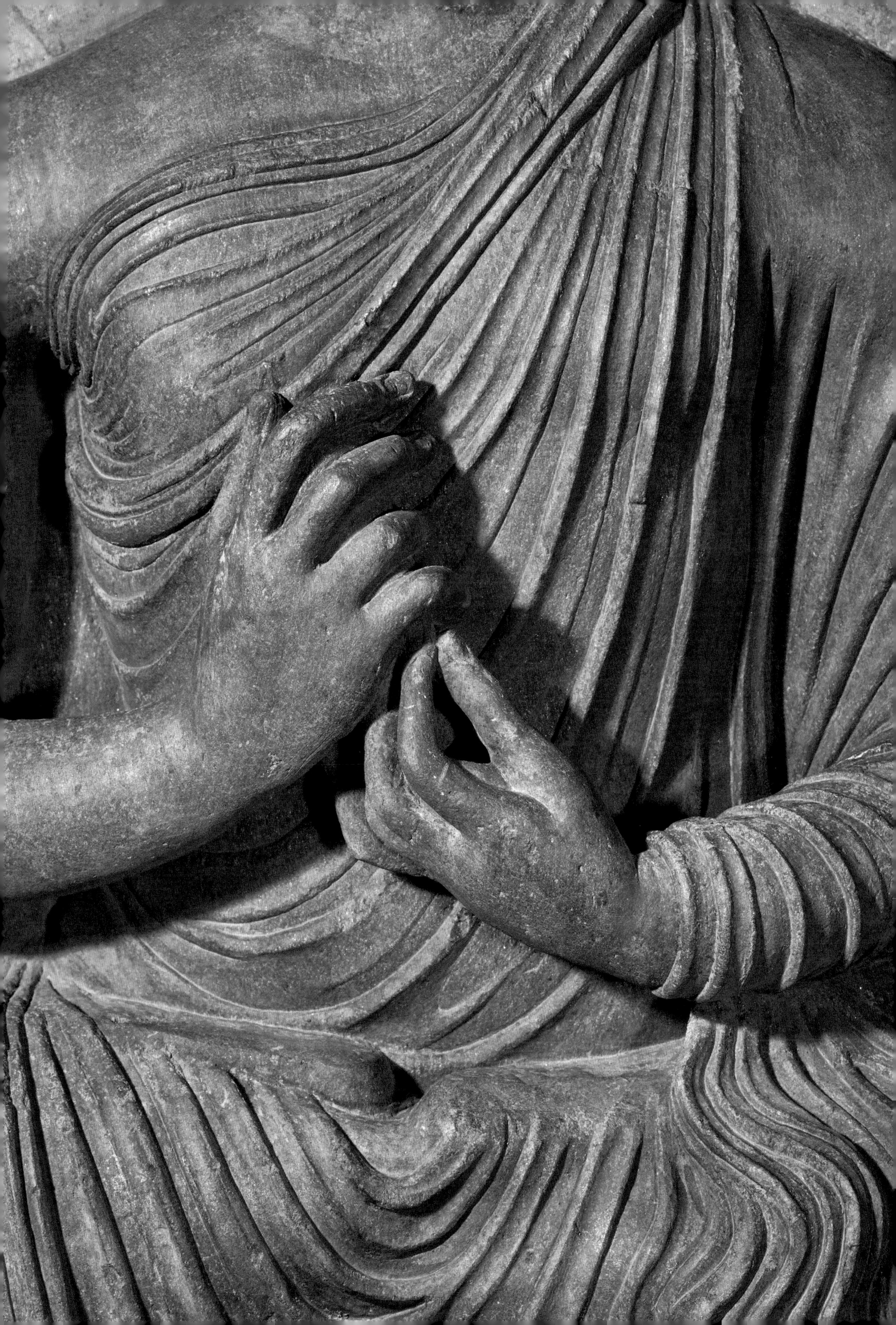

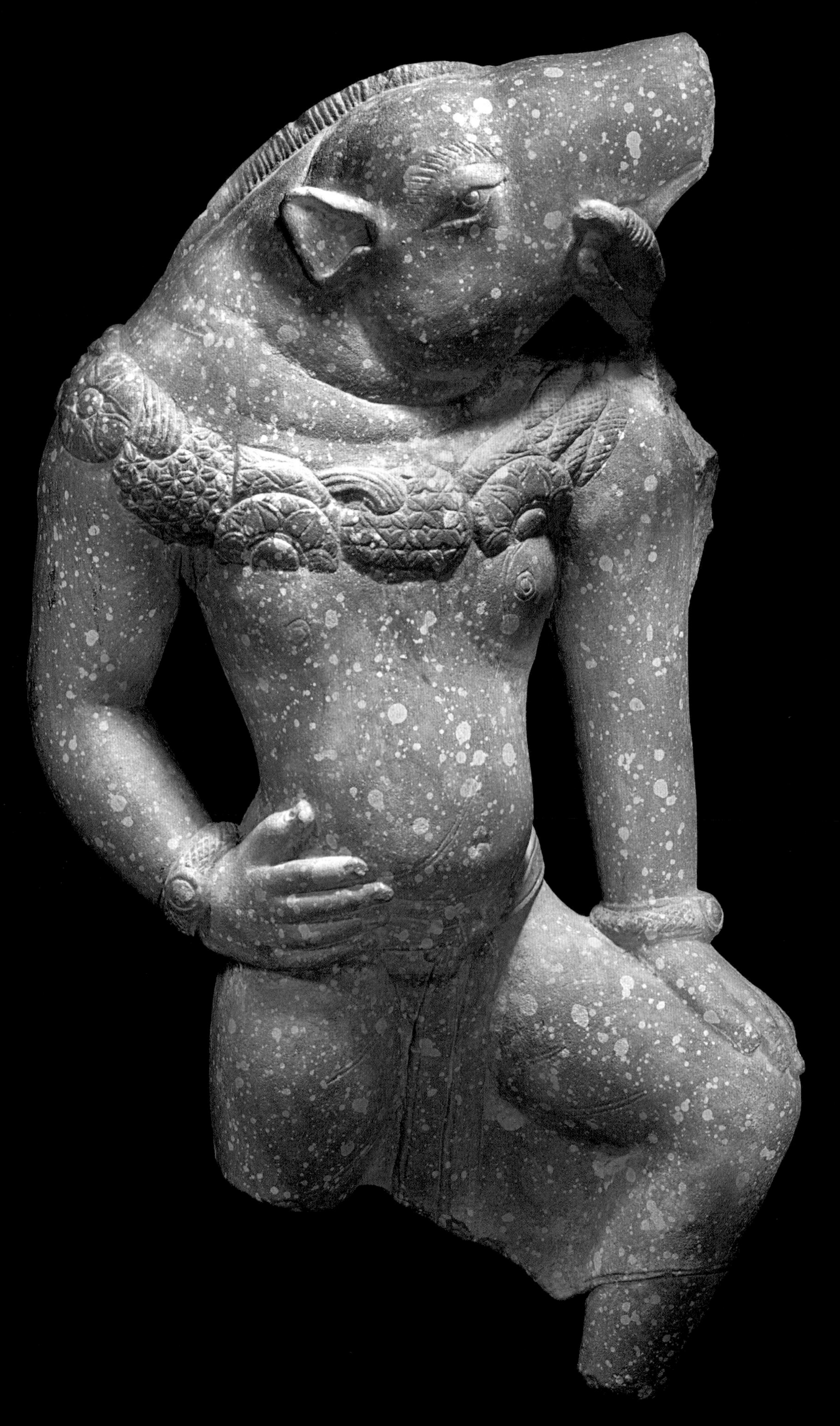

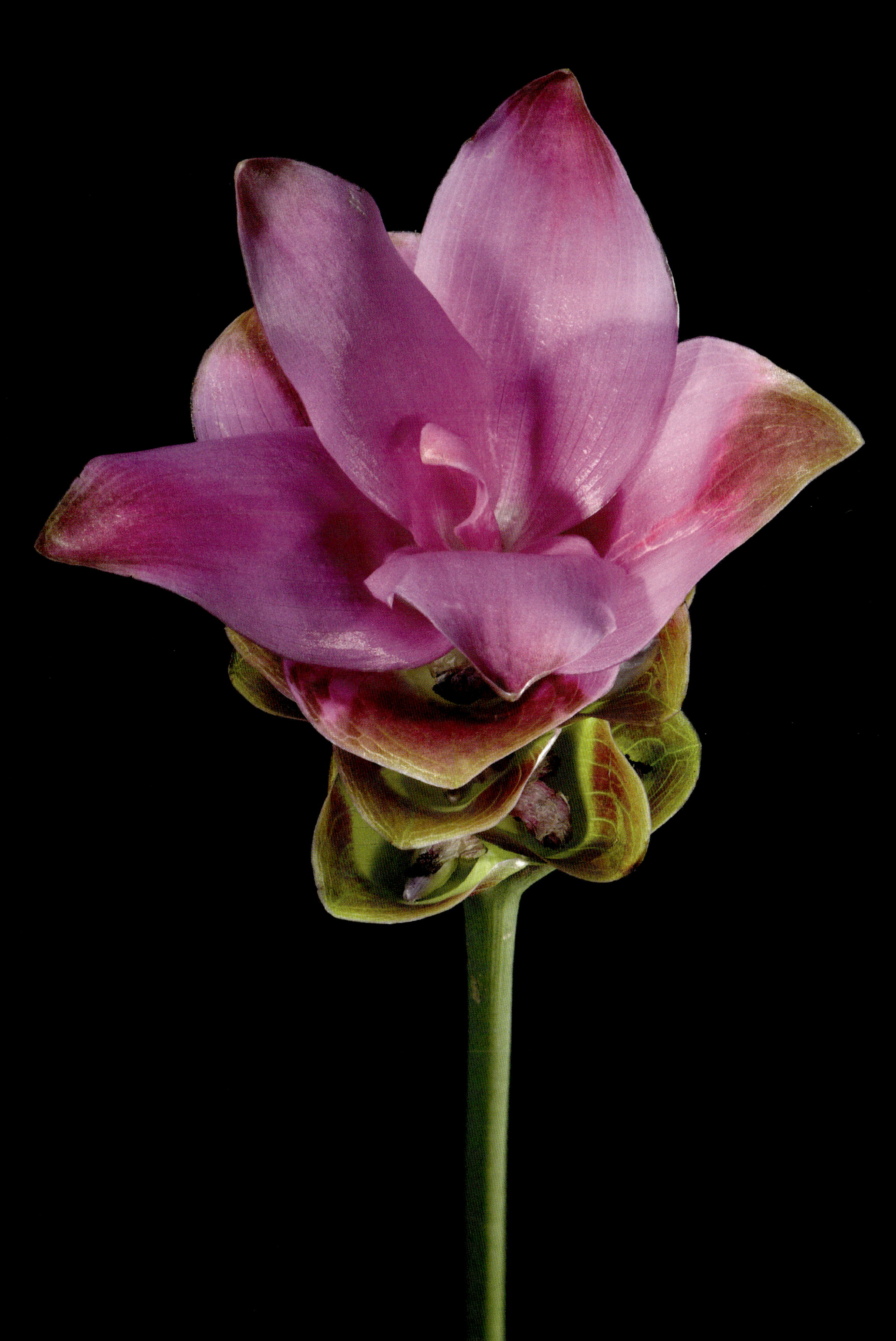

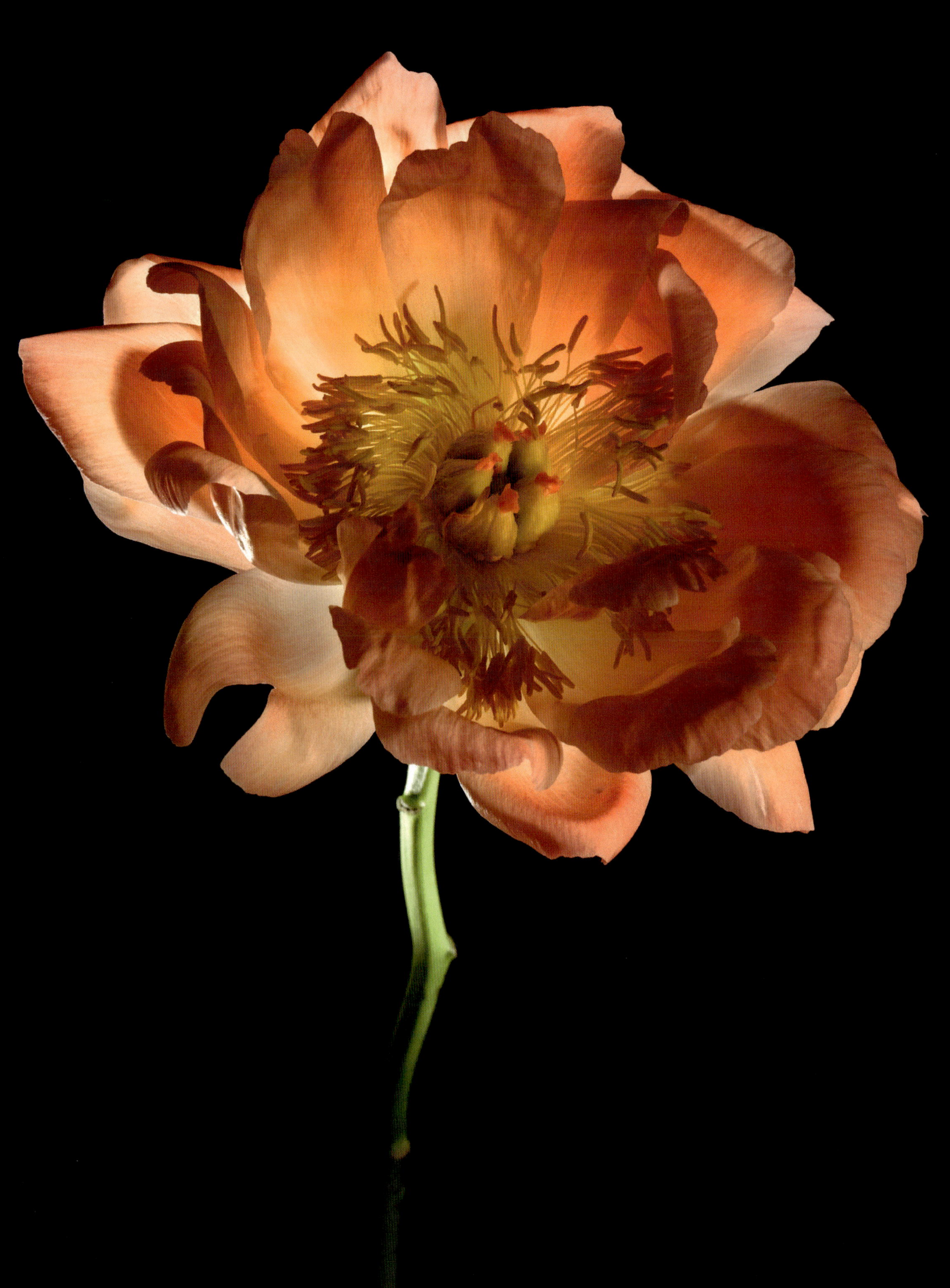

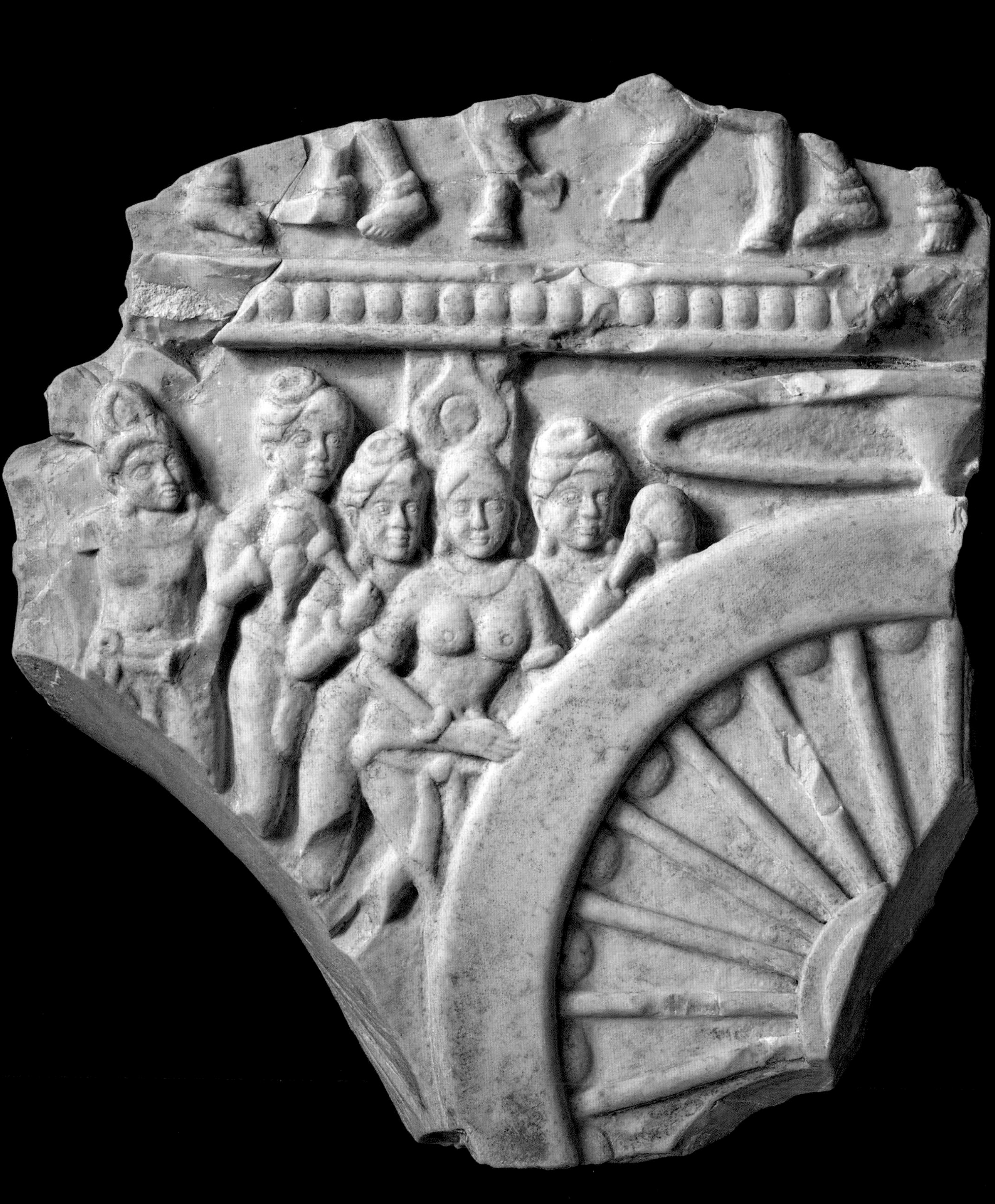

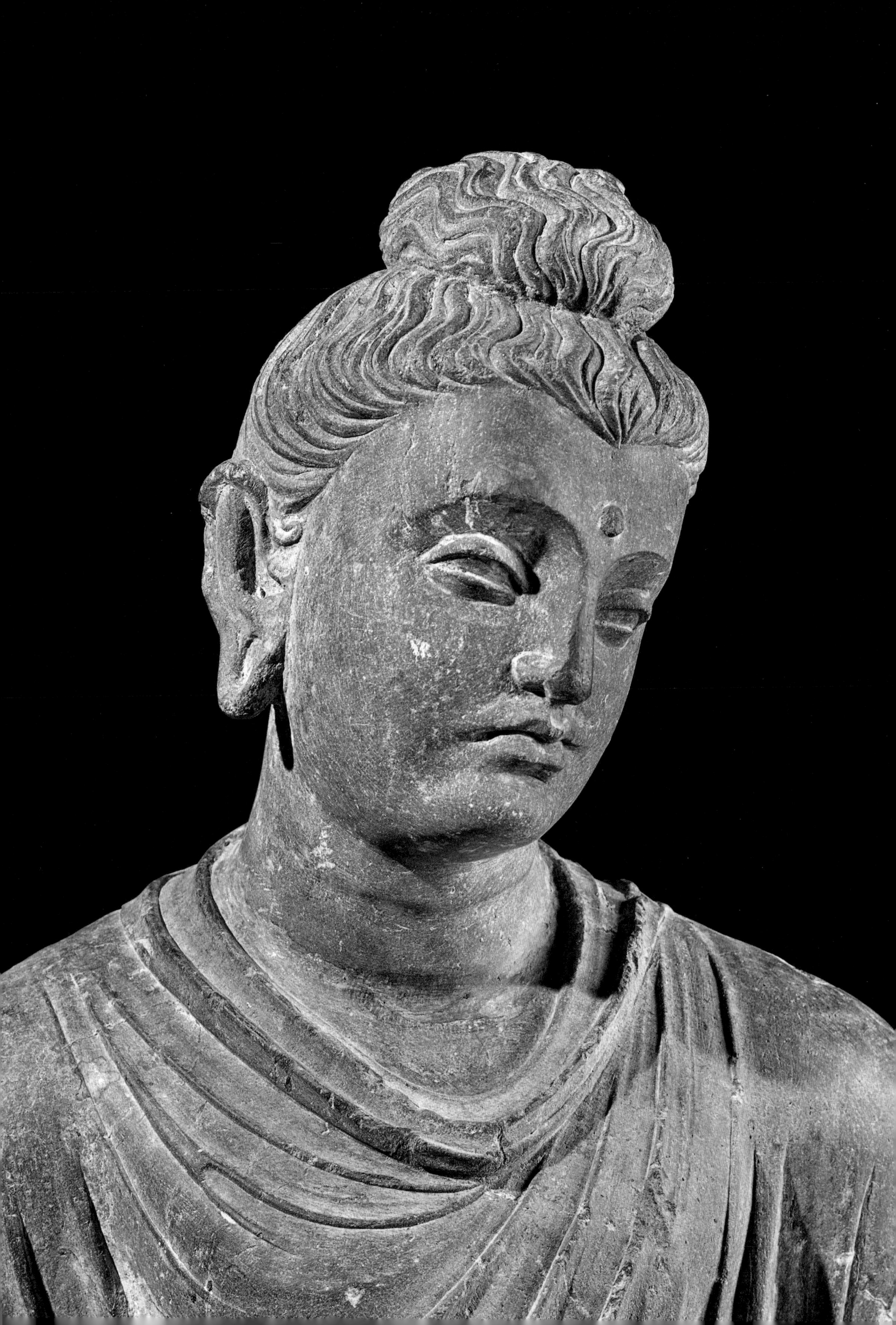

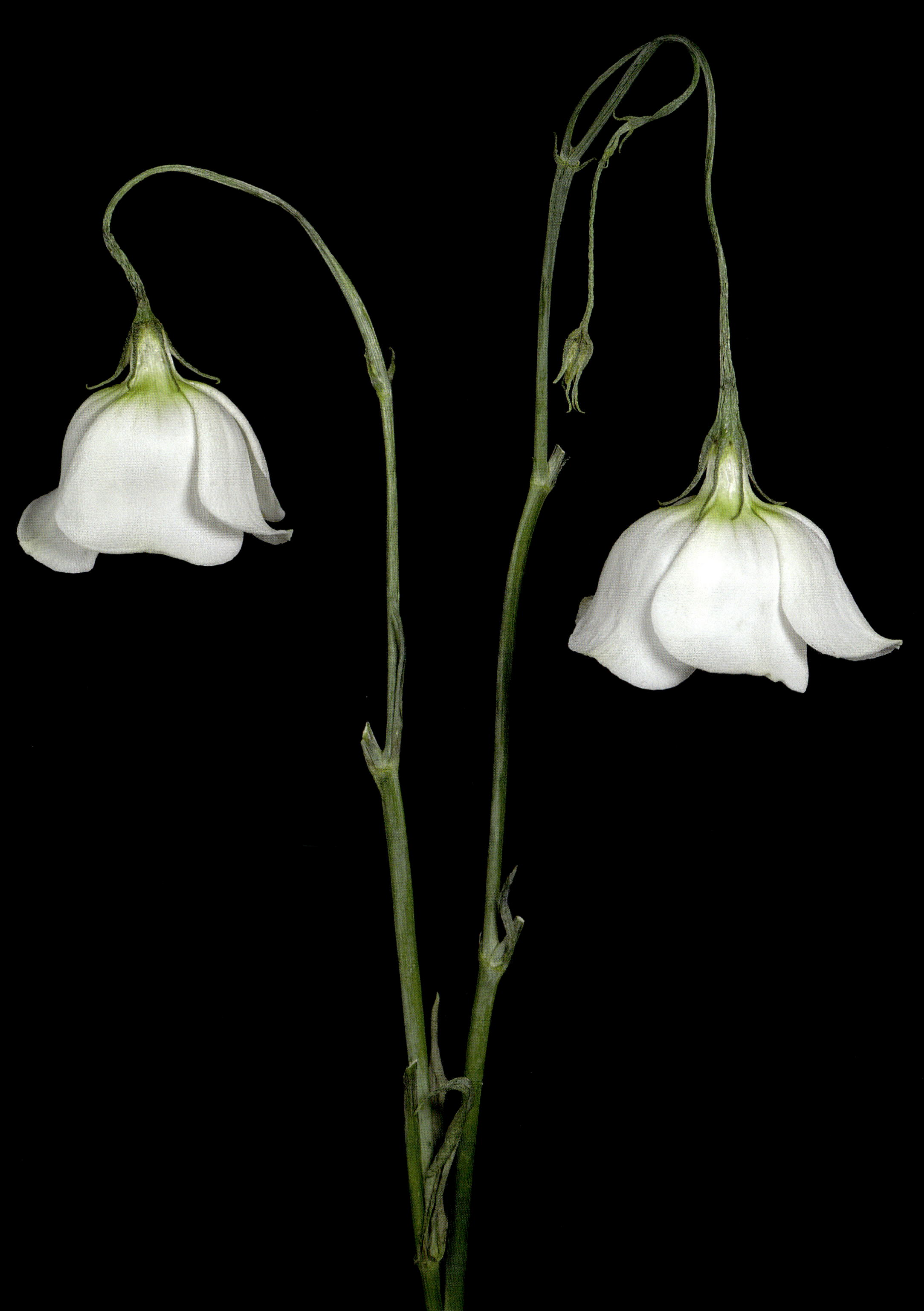

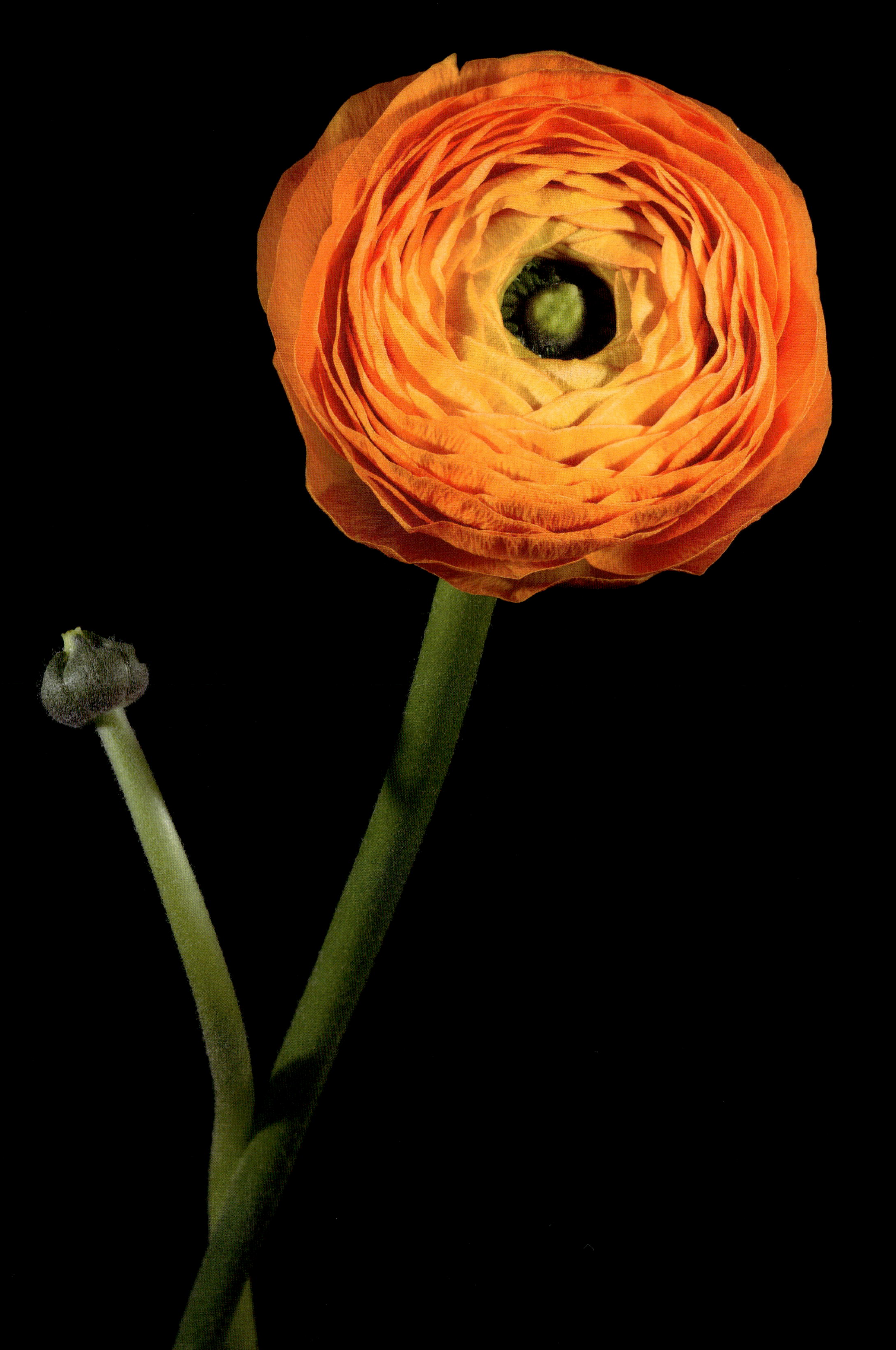

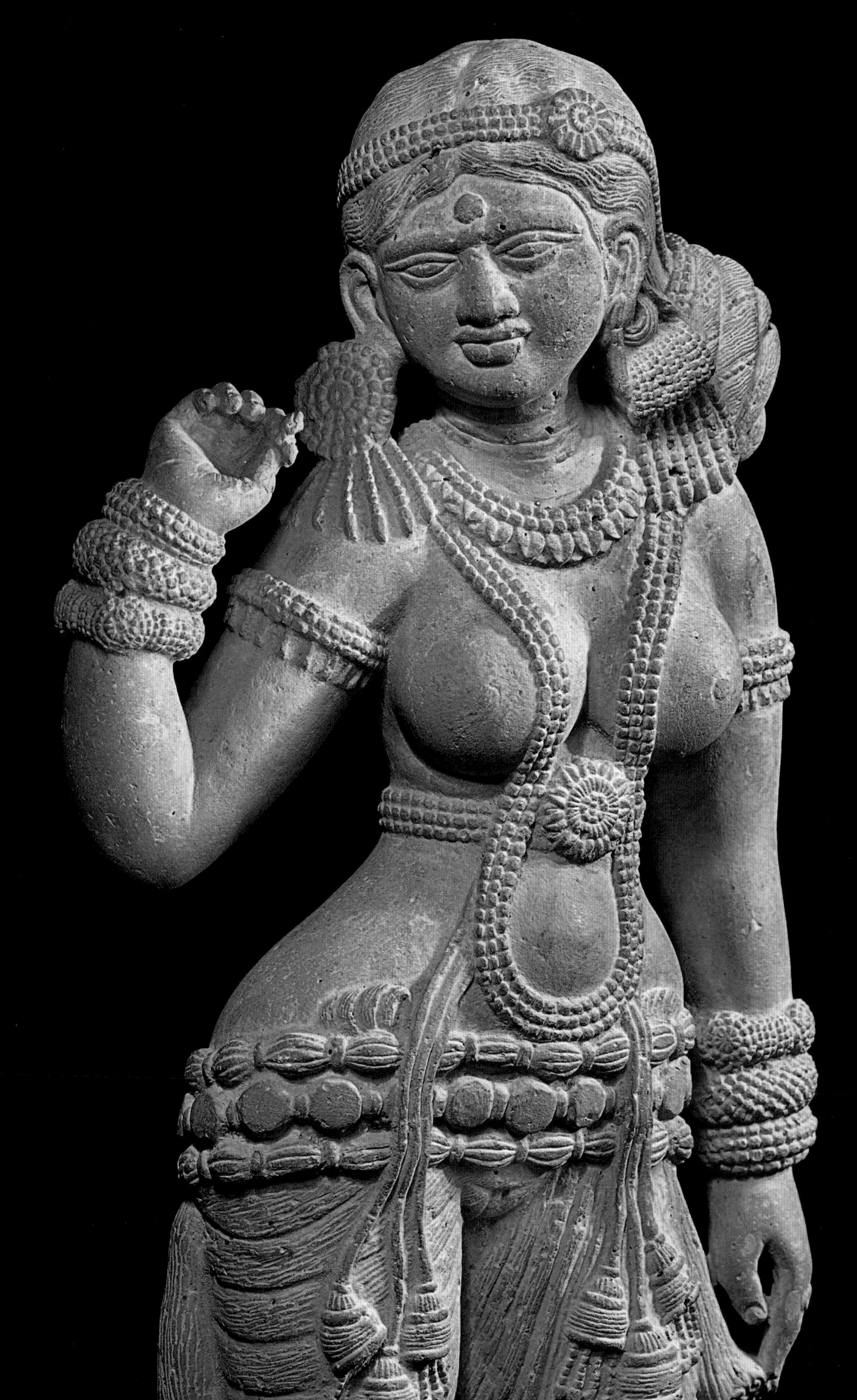

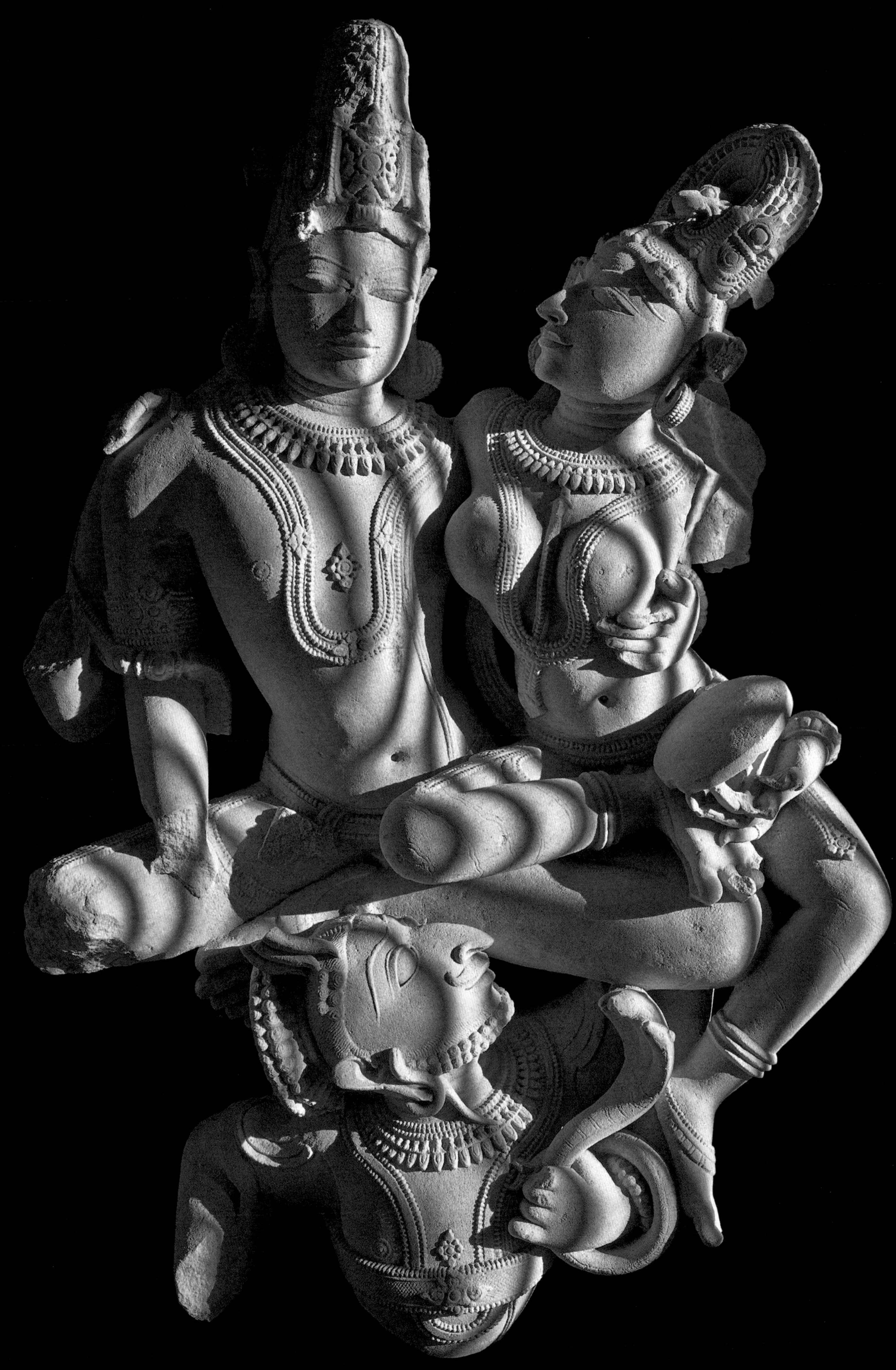

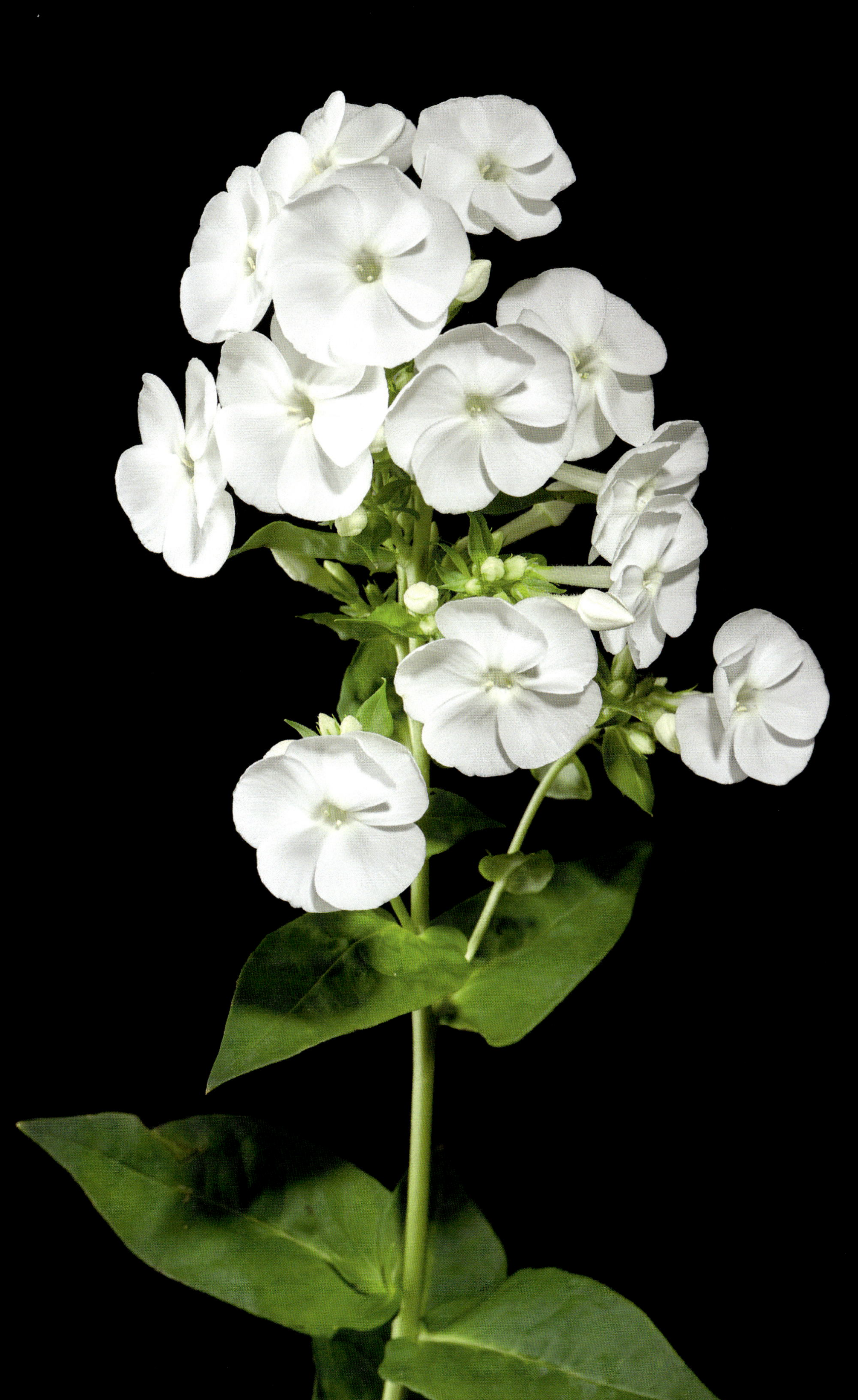

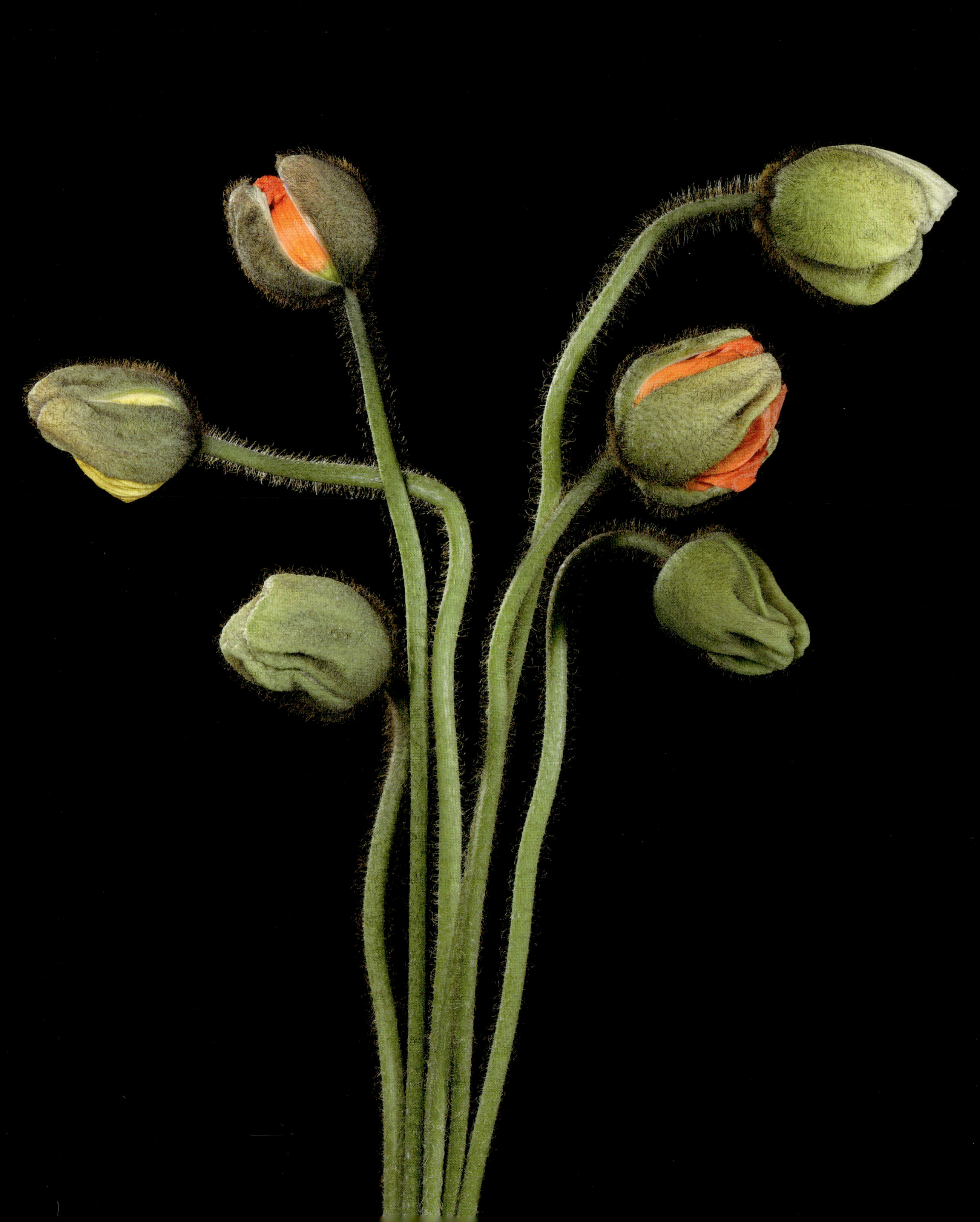

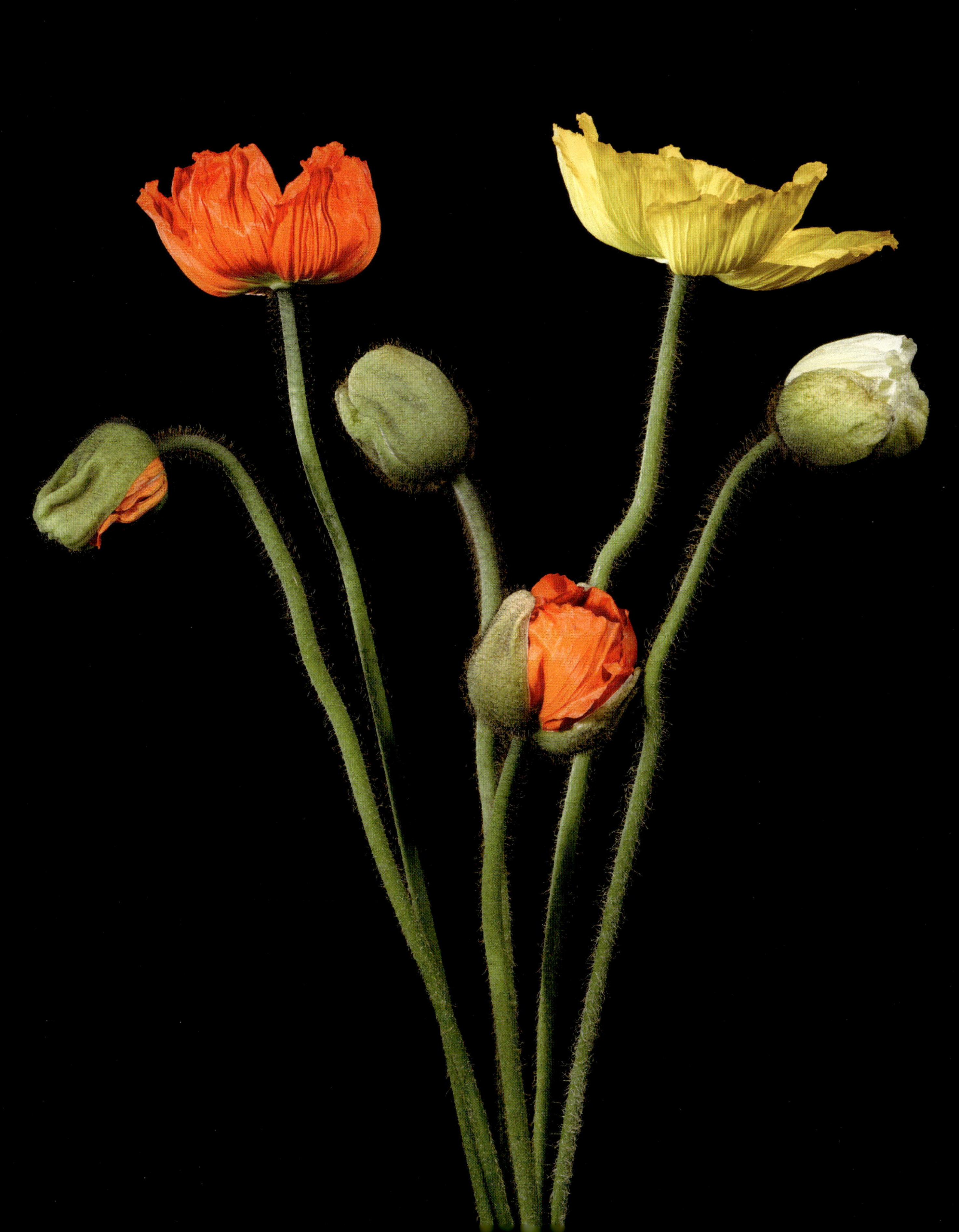

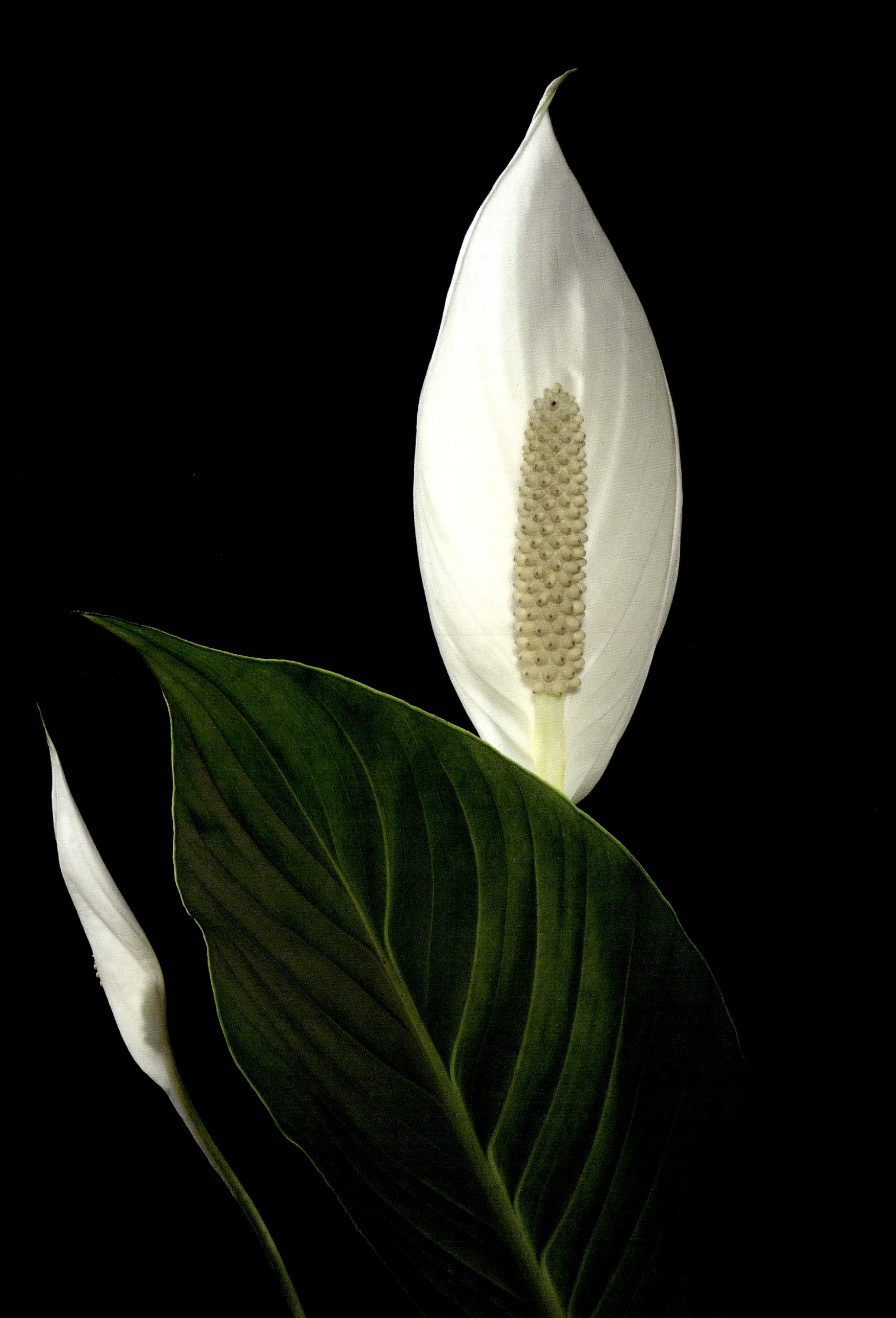

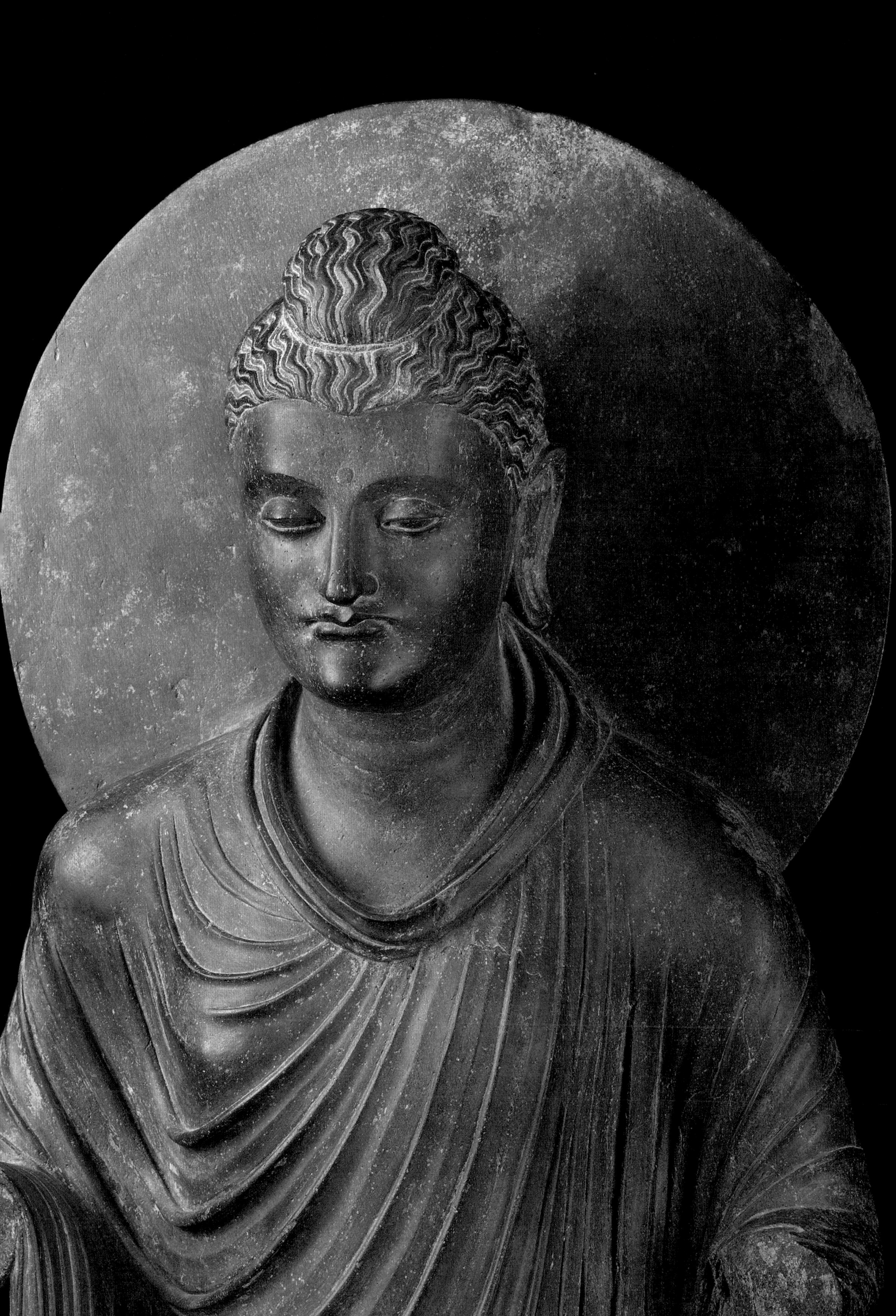

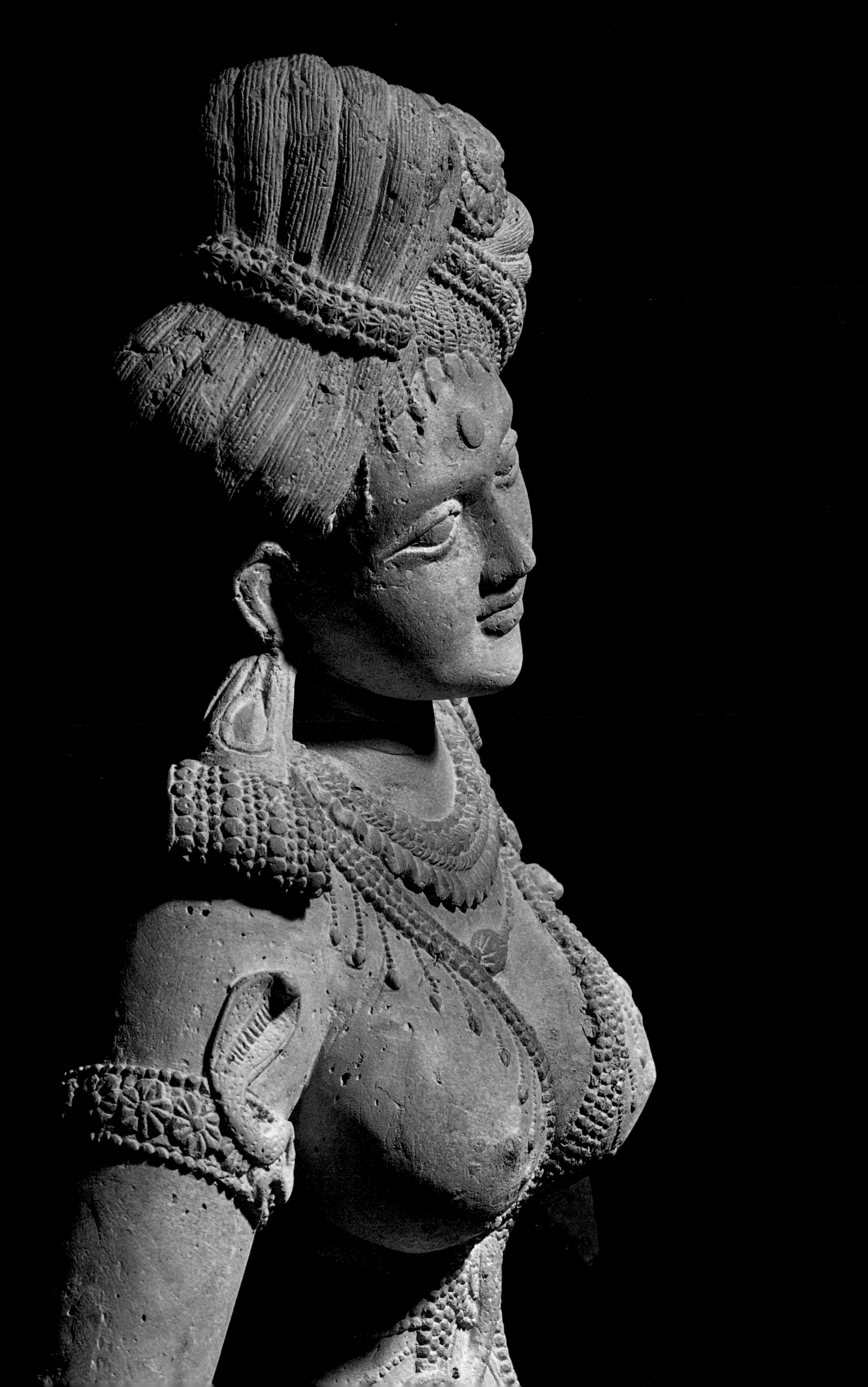

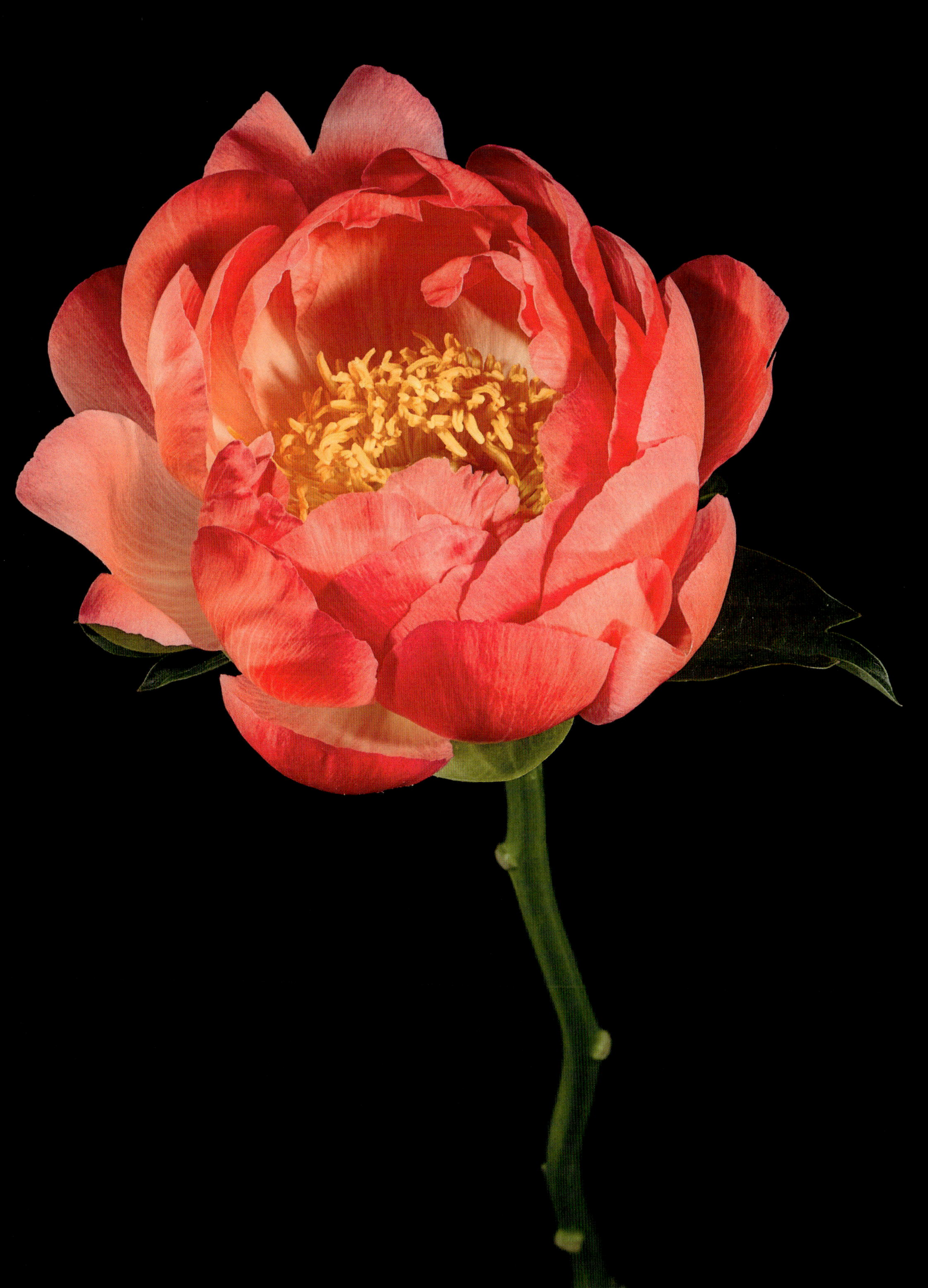

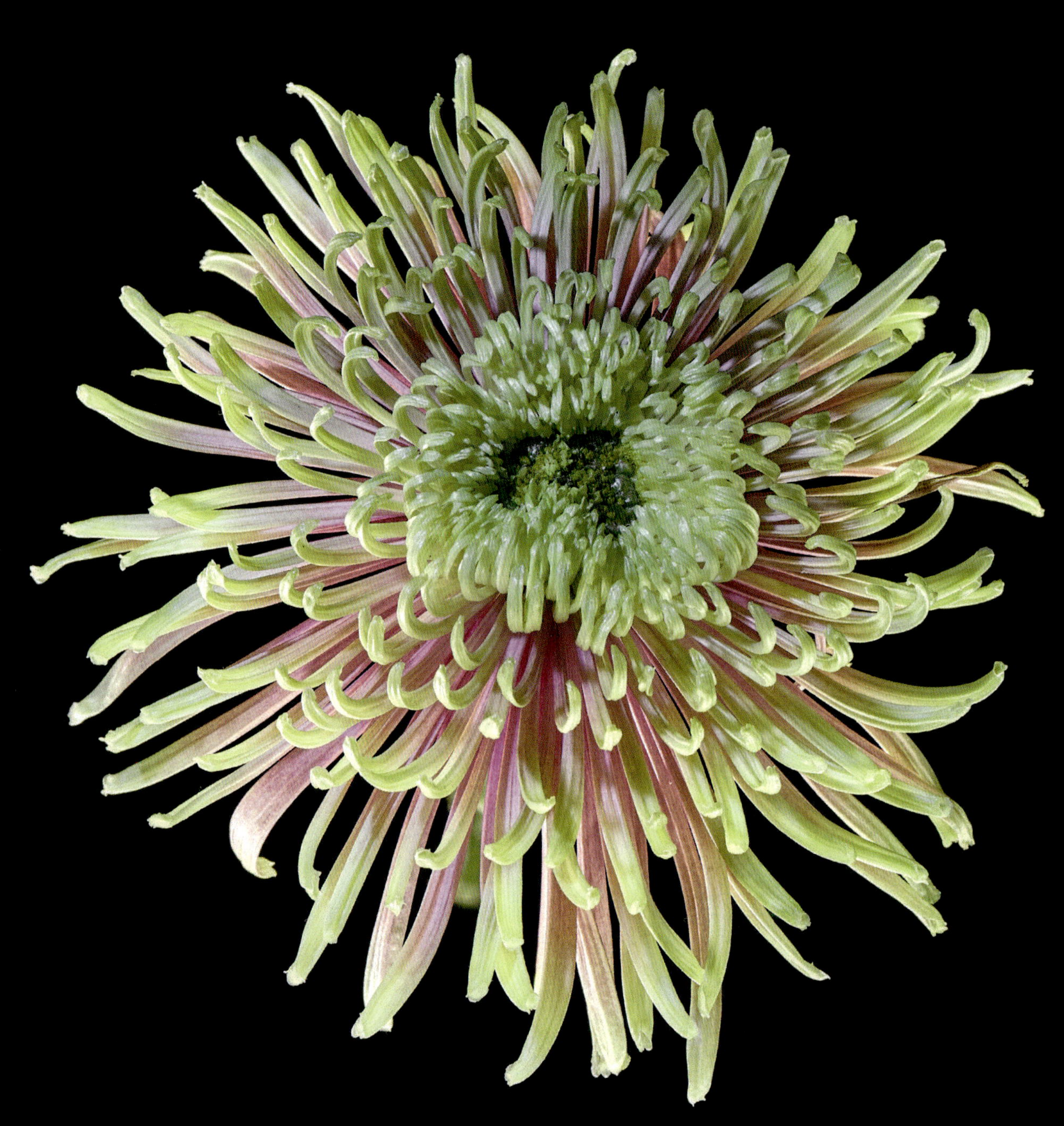

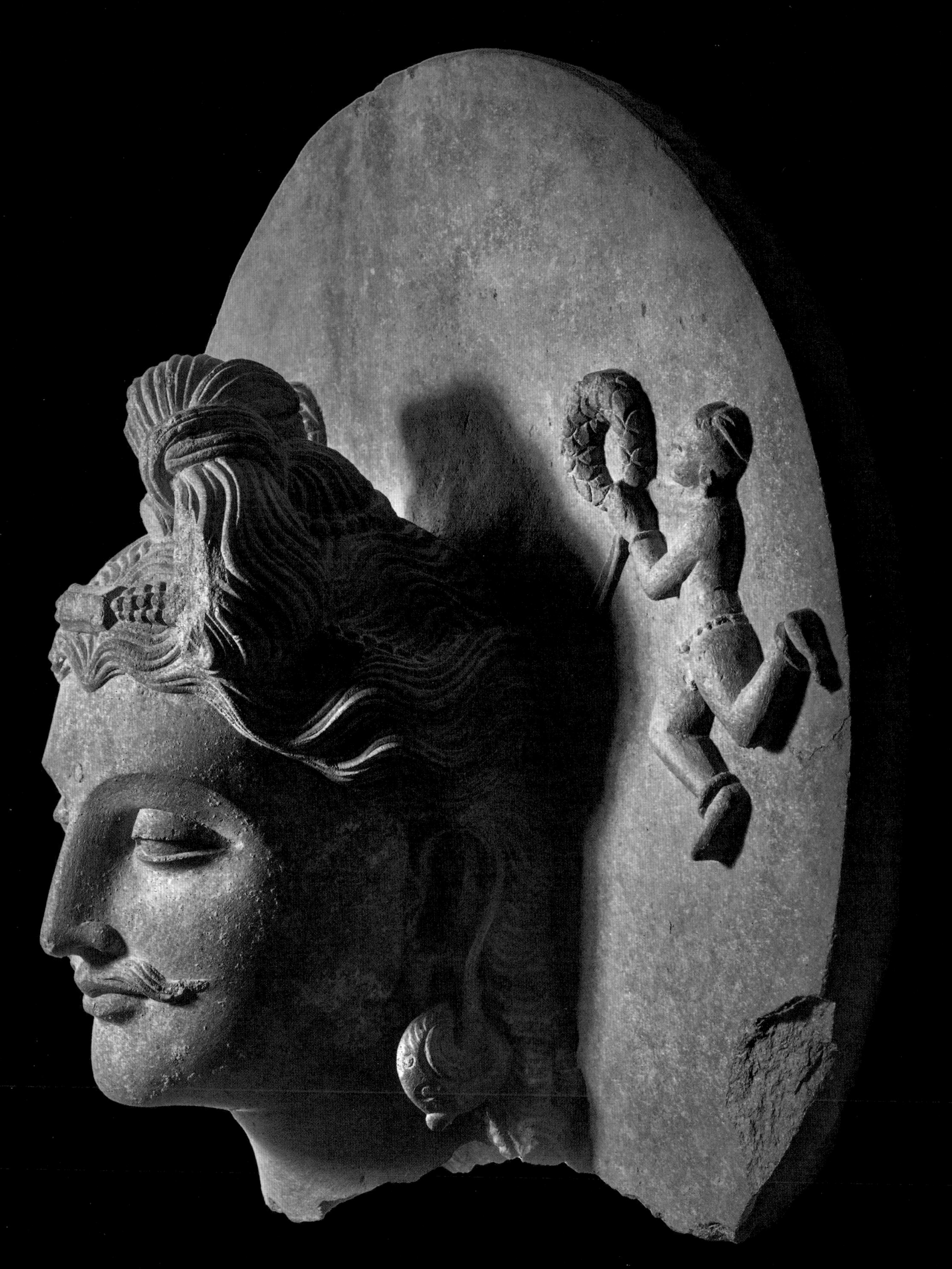

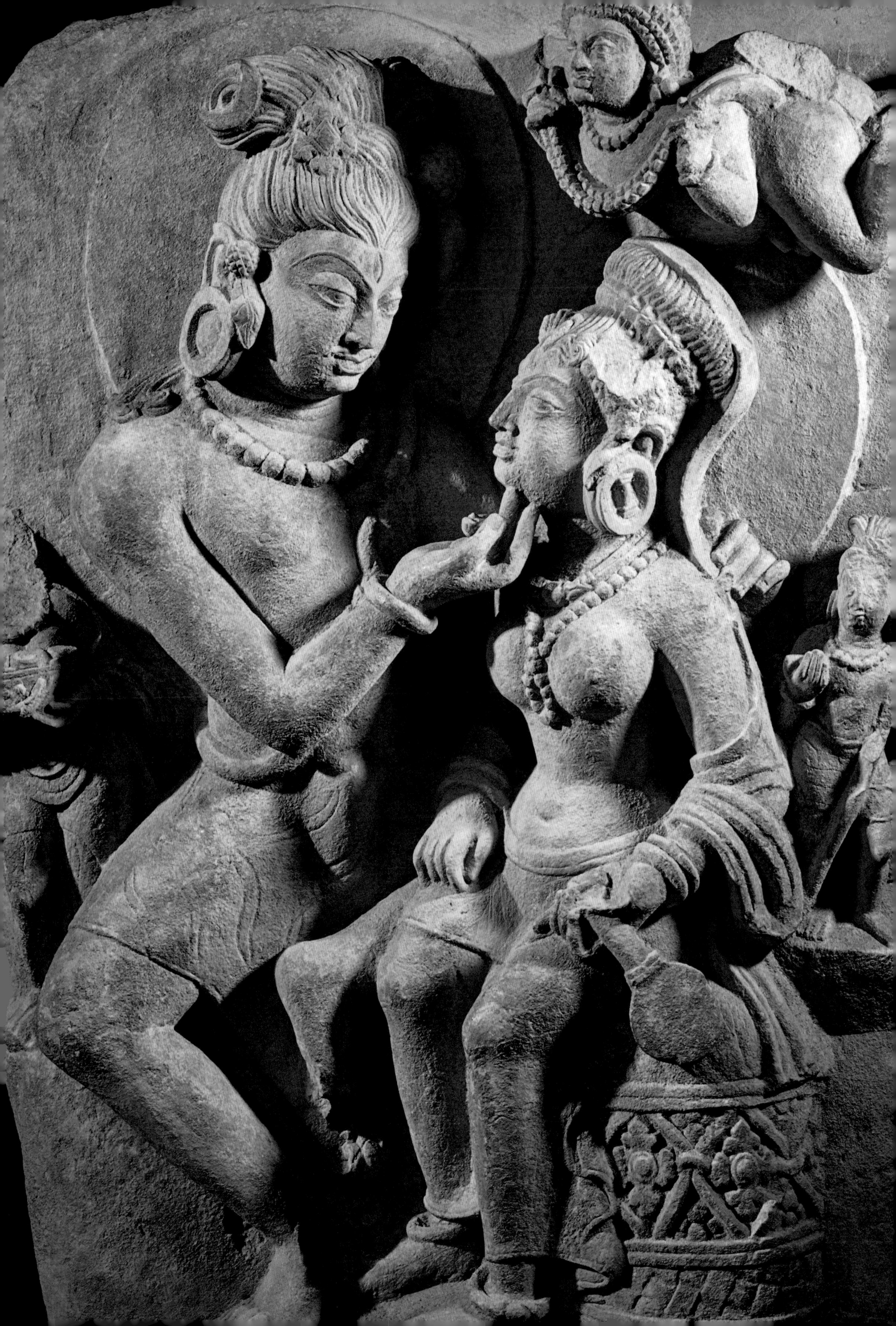

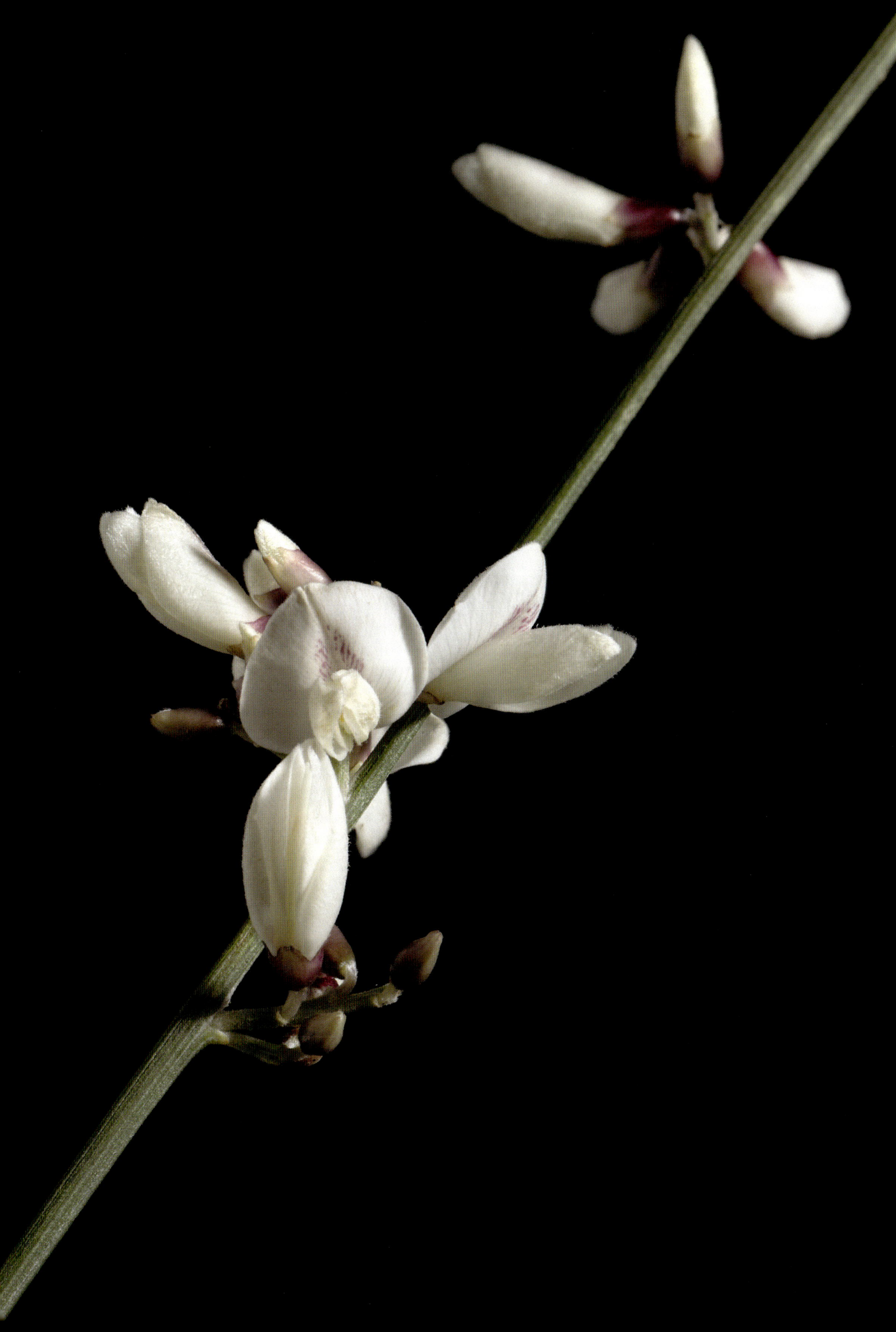

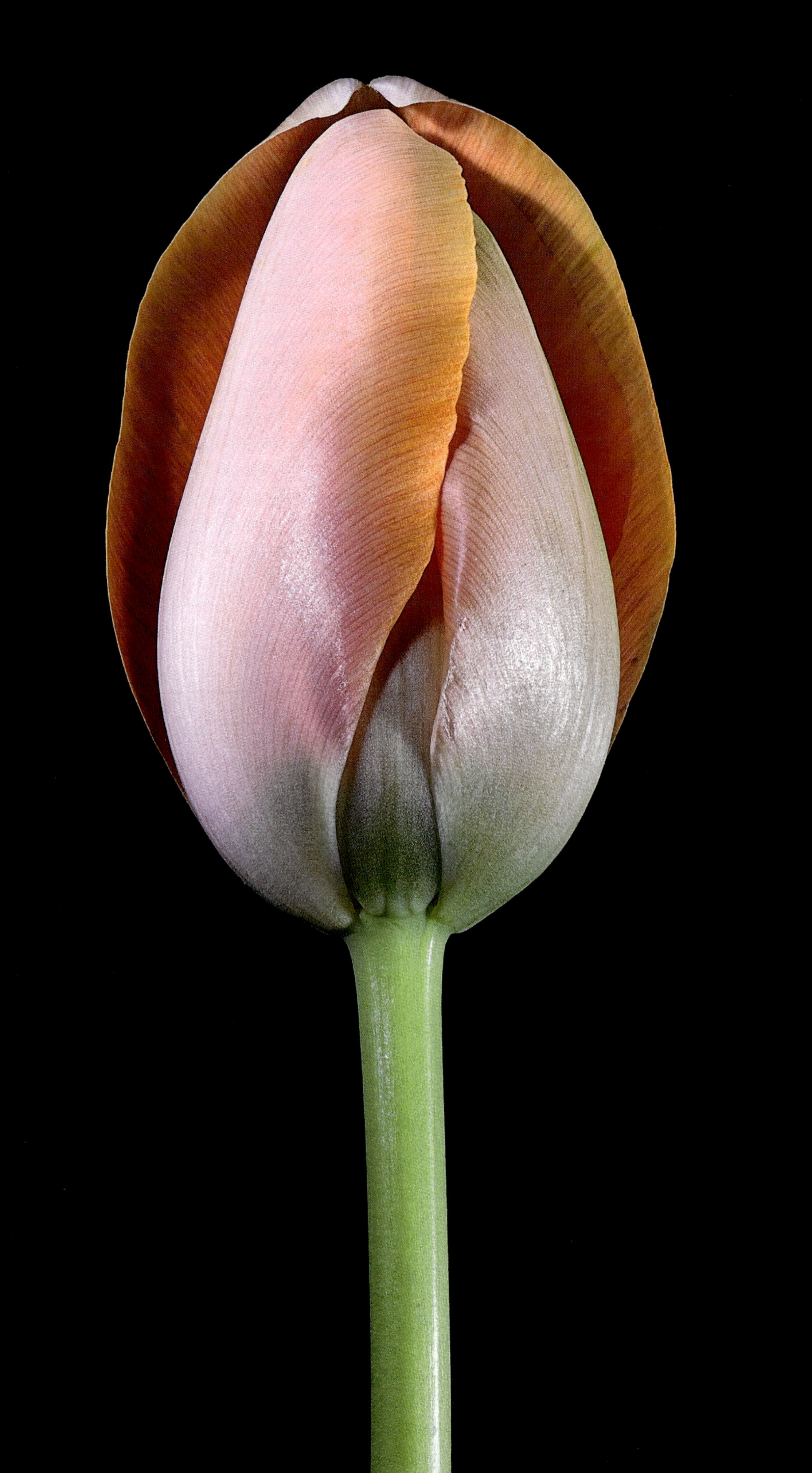

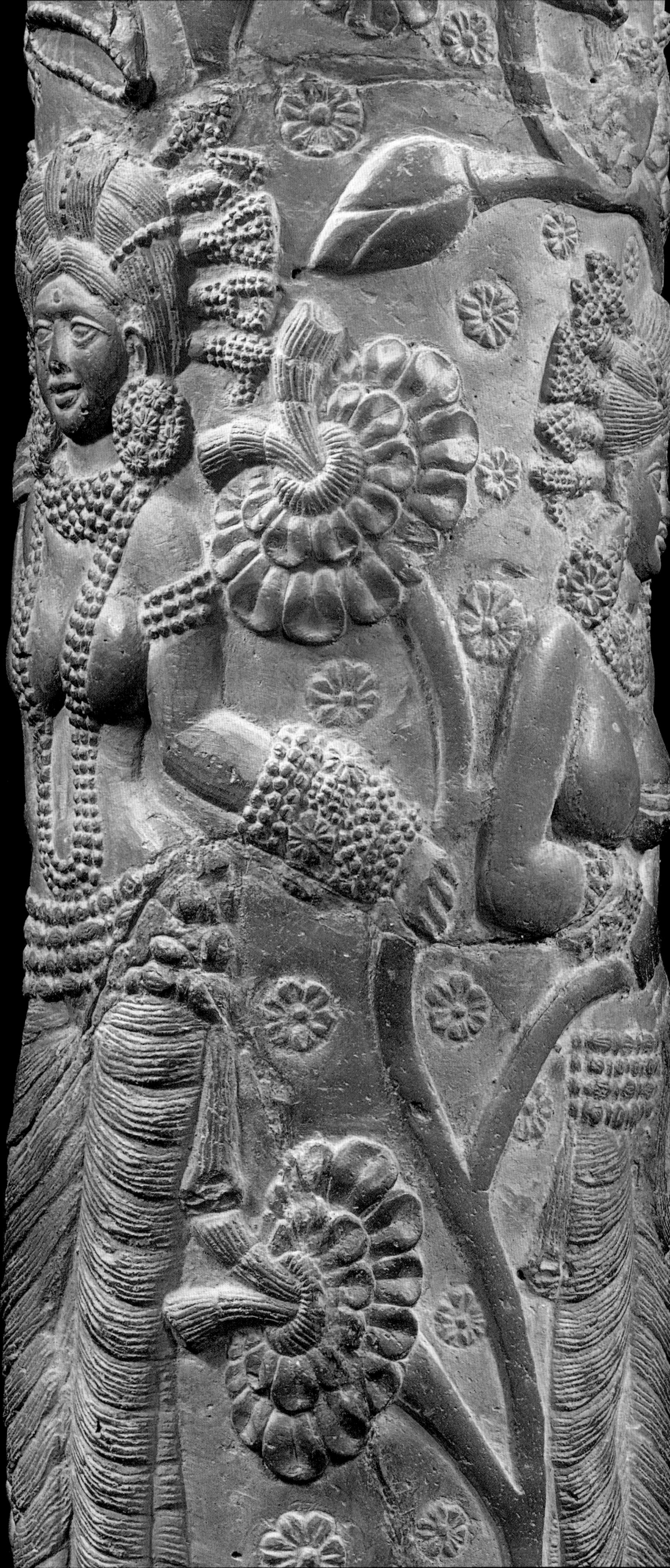

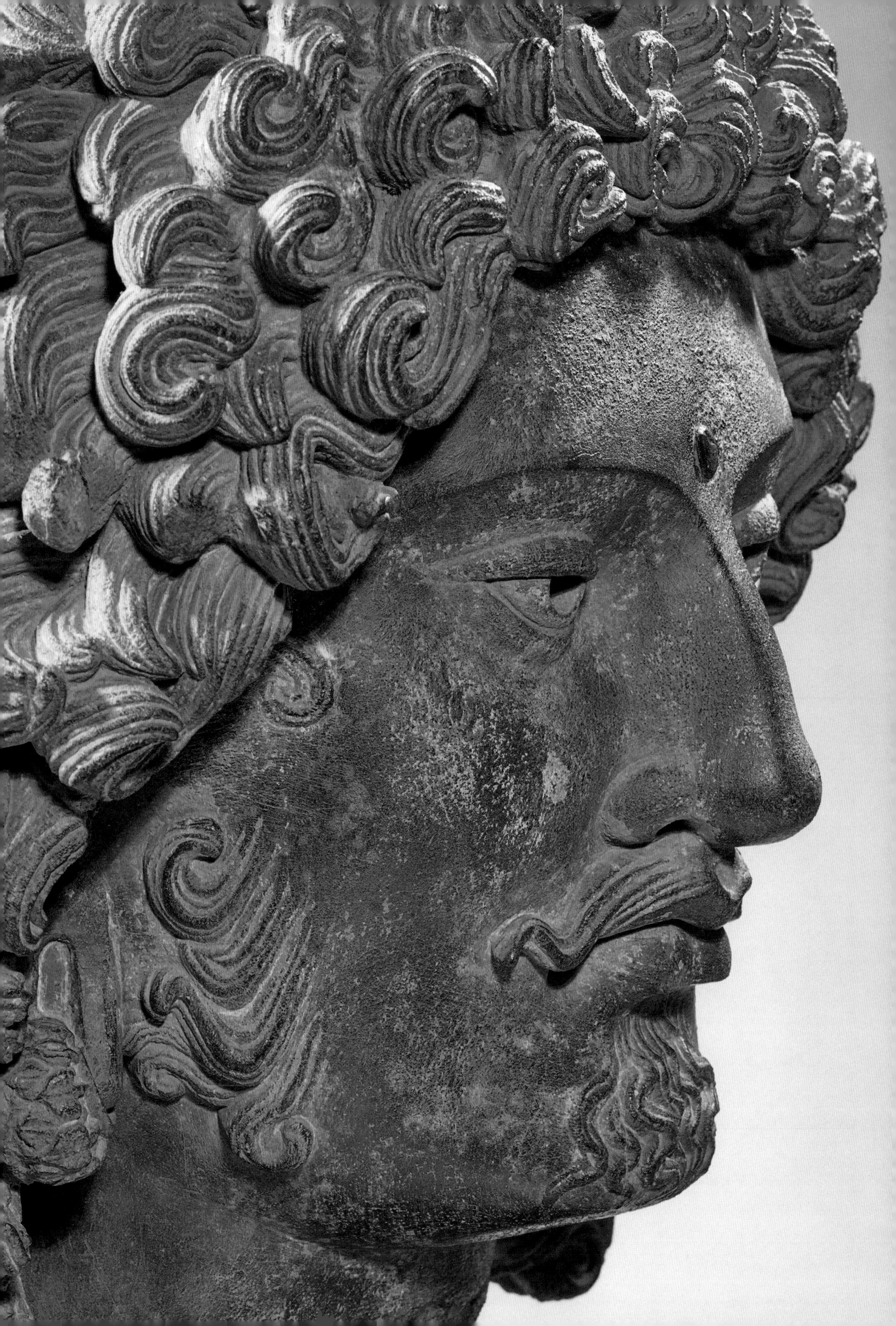

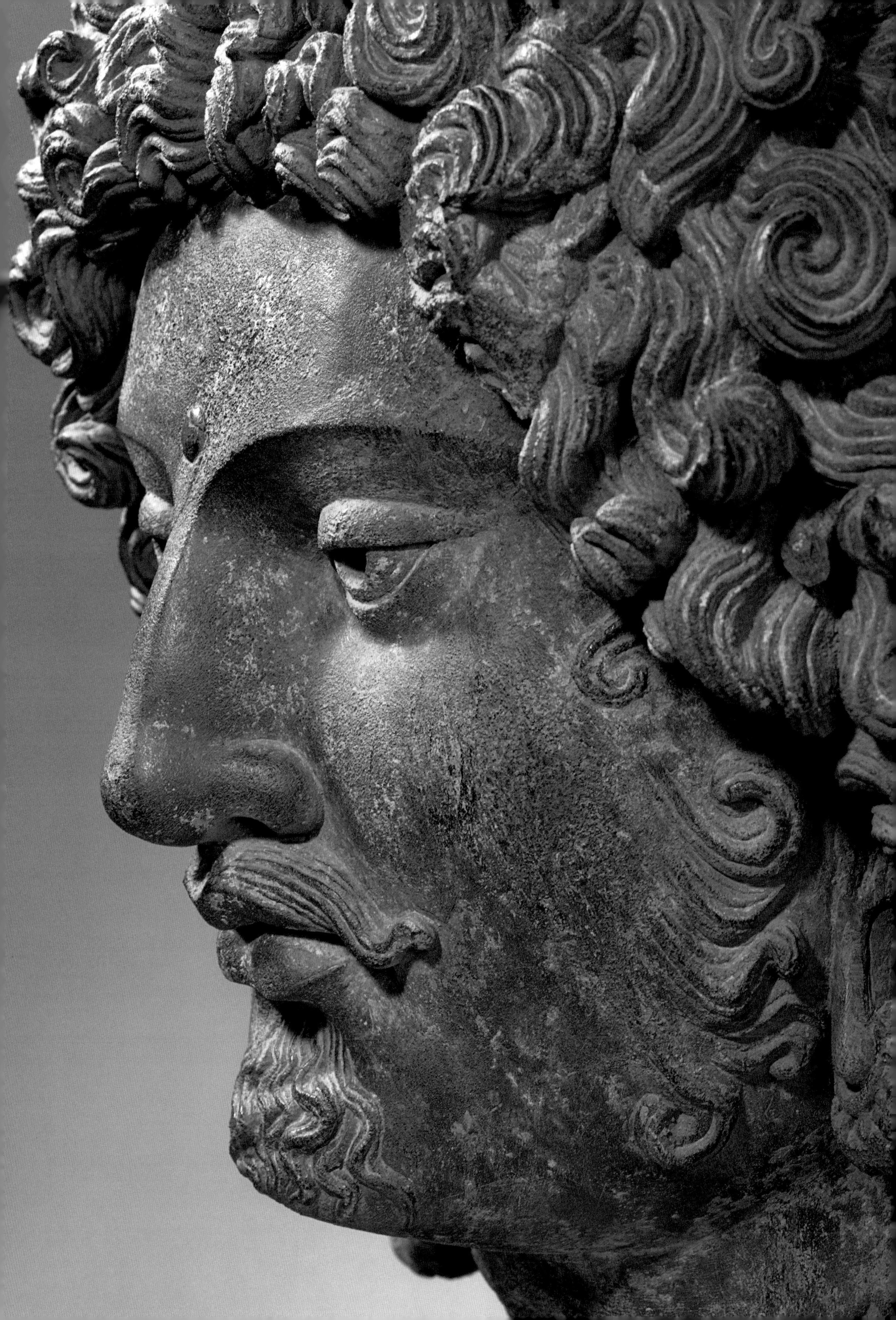

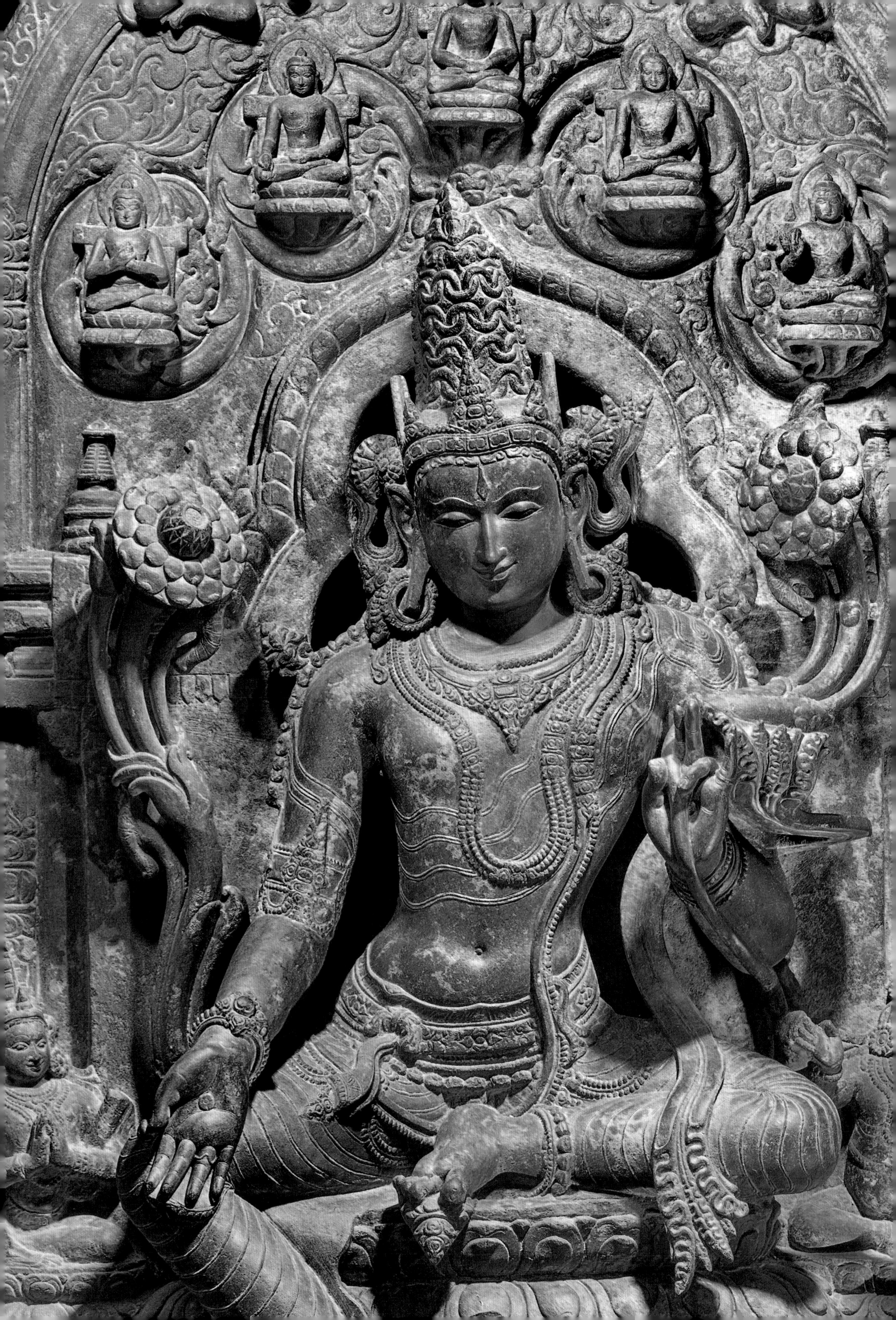

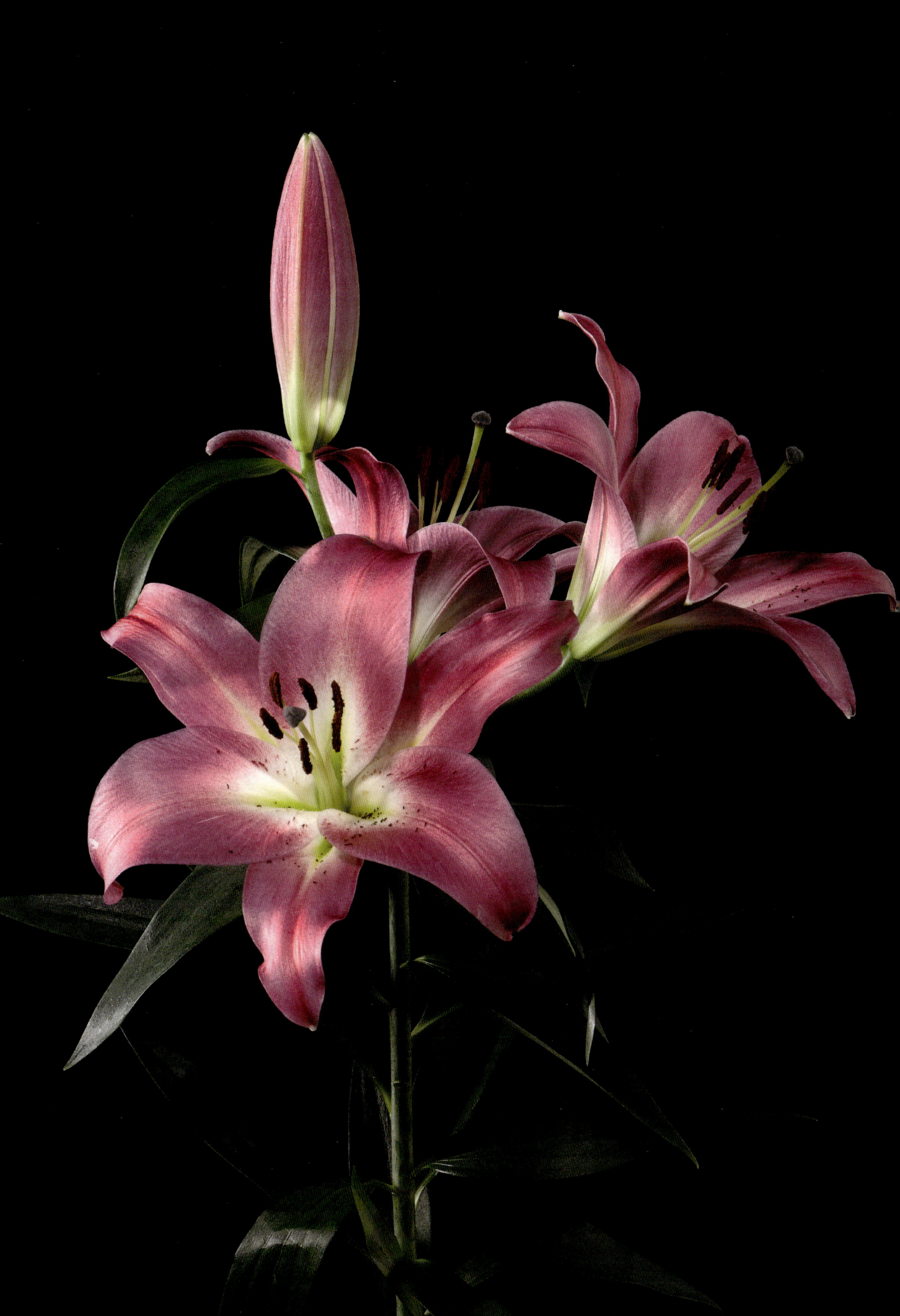

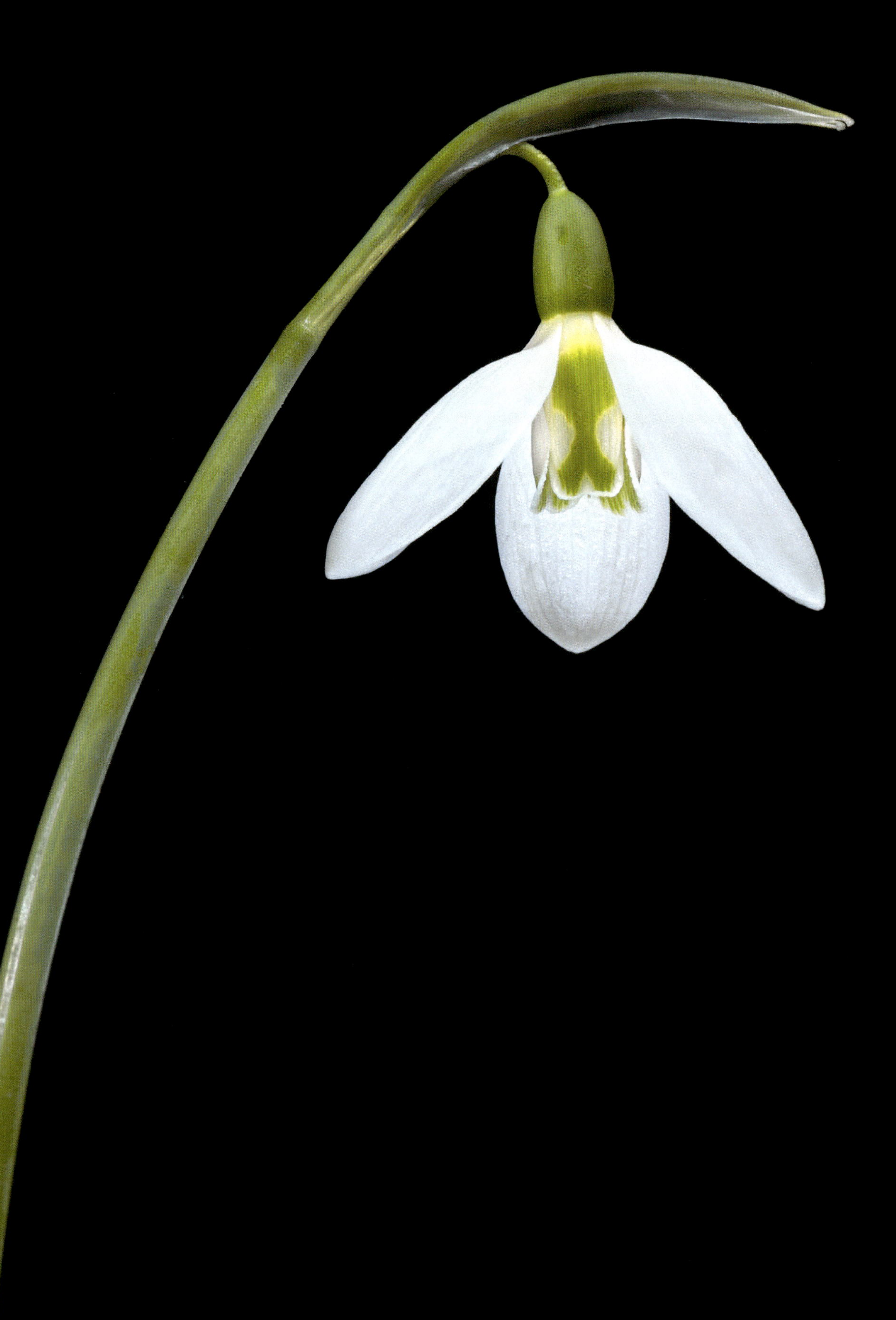

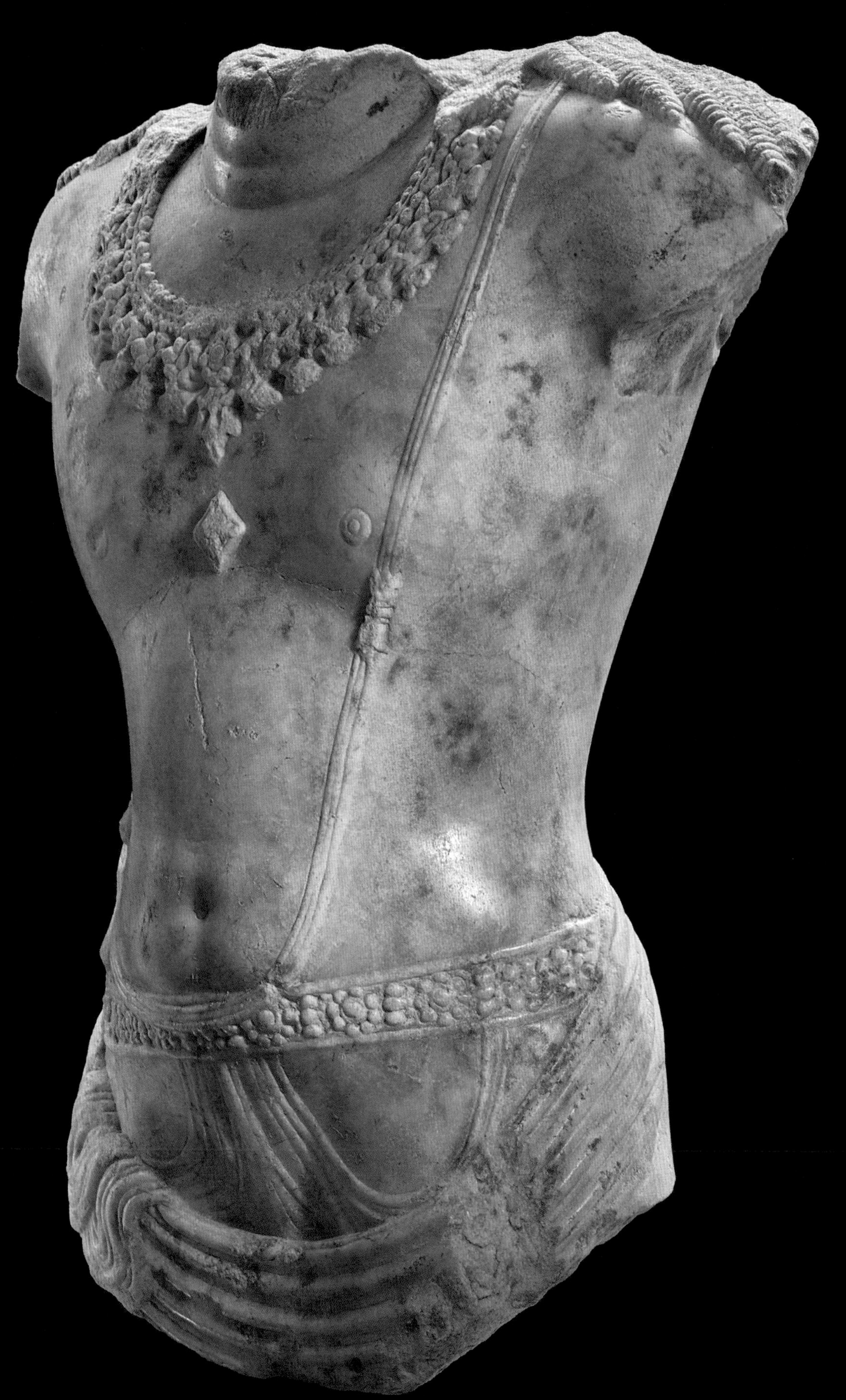

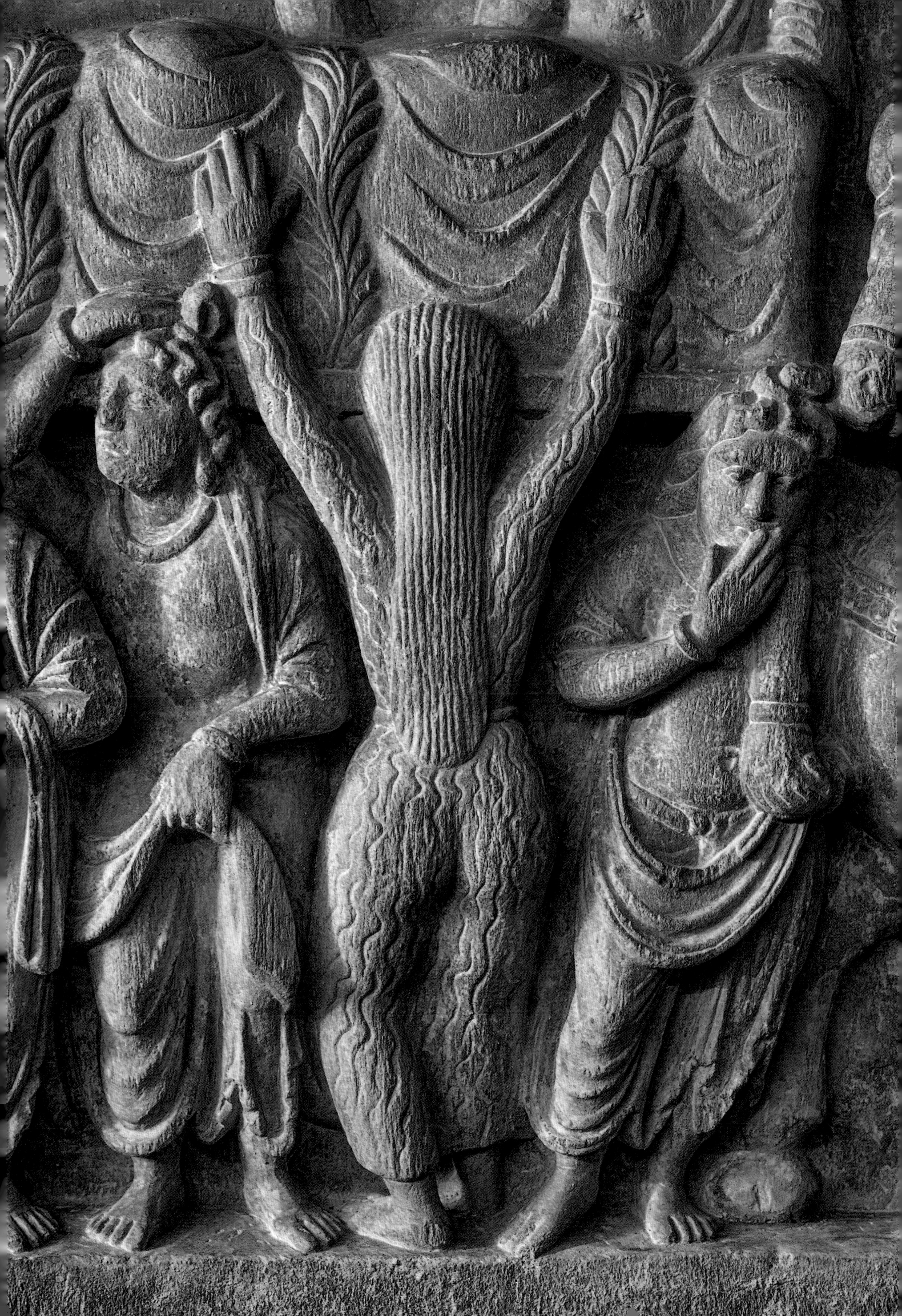

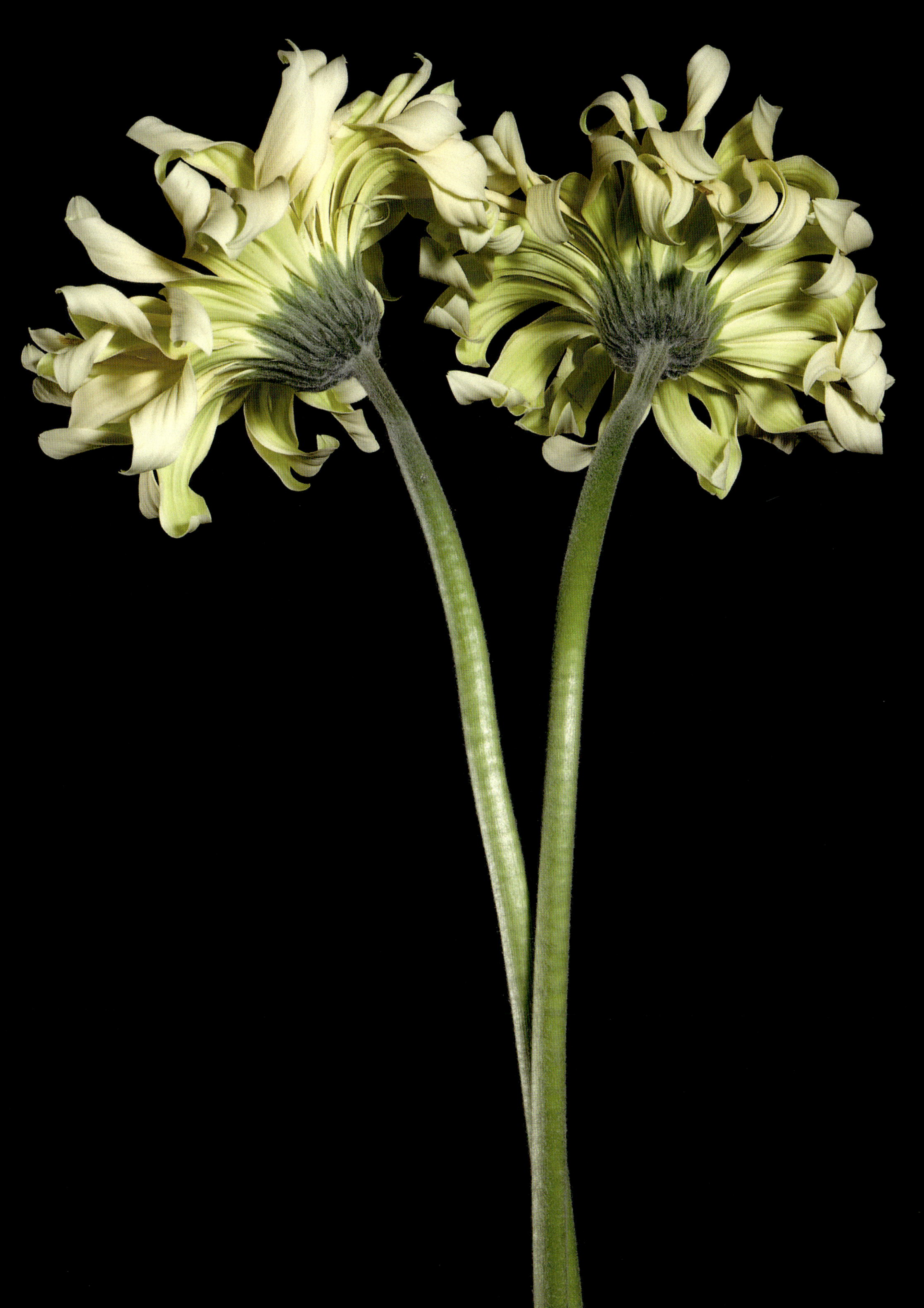

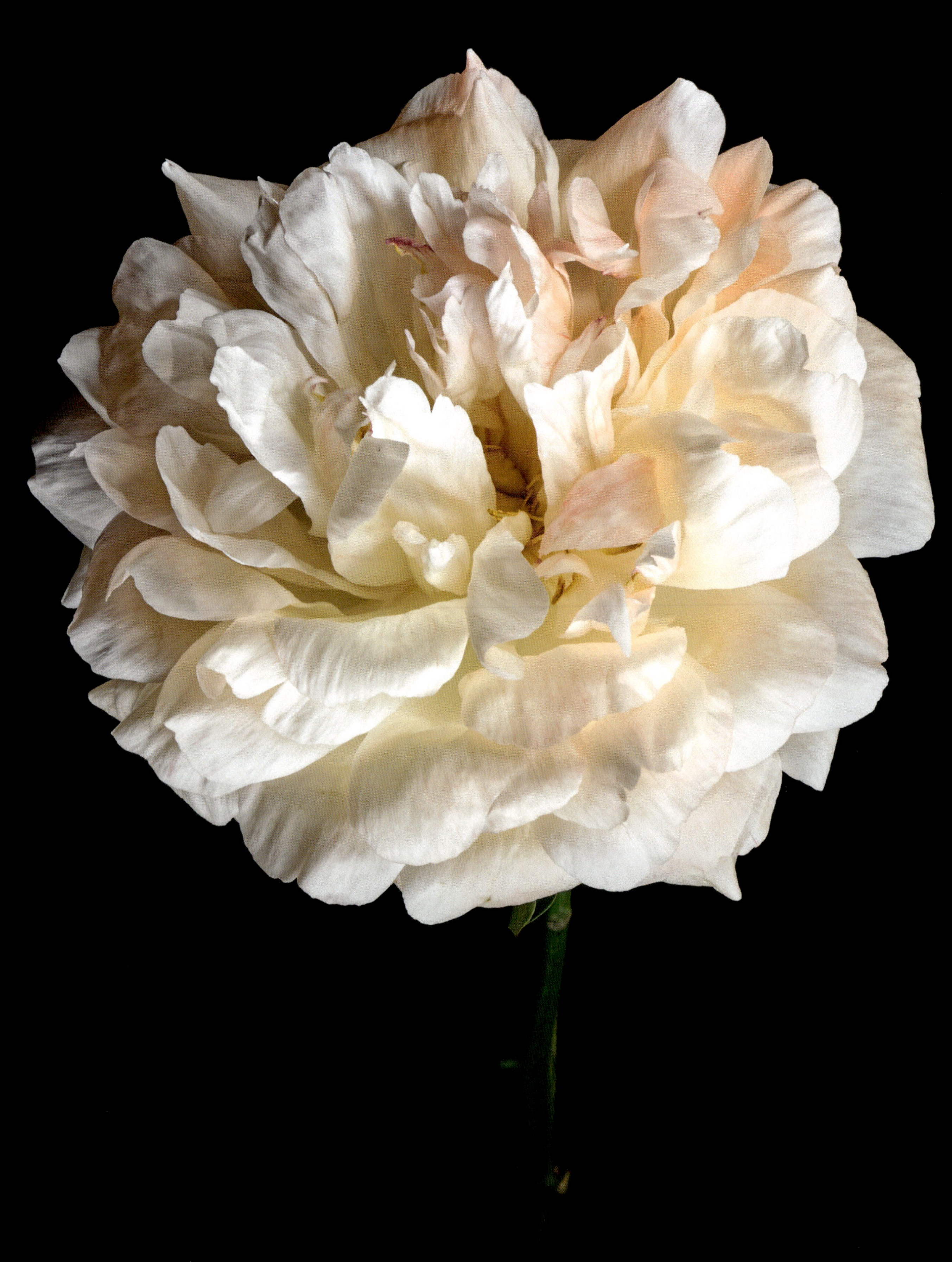

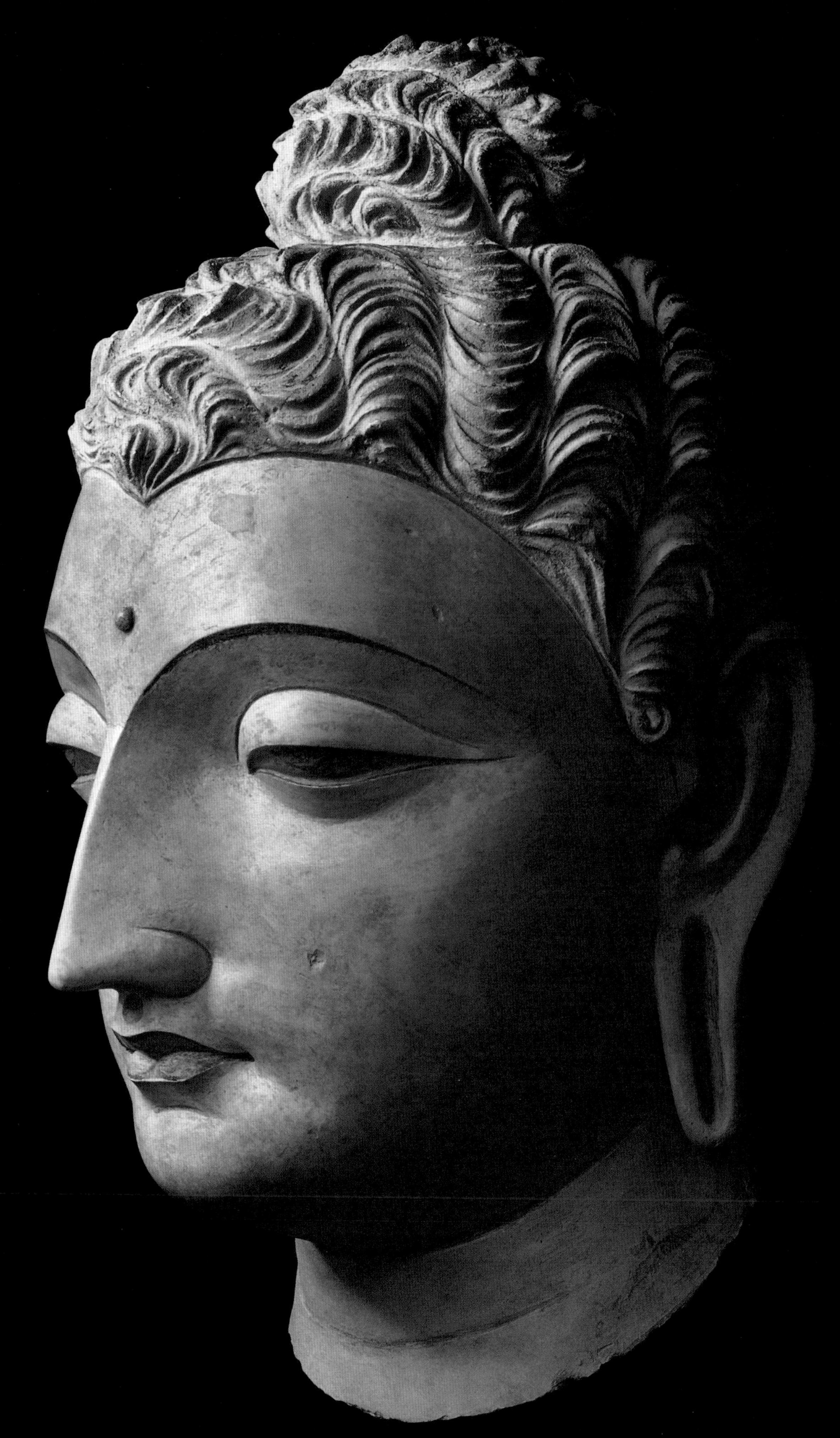

Index

SELECT BIBLIOGRAPHY

Acanthus History of Sculpture, The (in four volumes)
 (London: the Oldbourne Press, 1960-62)

Blochwitz, Daniel in *René Groebli: The Magic Eye*
 (Zurich: Edition Bildhalle, 2019) · For the quote, see page 3.

Campany, David; 'Irving Penn's Flowers' in Irving Penn, *Flowers*
 (London: Hamilton's Gallery, 2015) · For the quote, see page 5.

von Goethe, Johann Wolfgang; *The Metamorphosis of Plants*
 (Cambridge: The MIT Press, 2009; first published 1790)

von Goethe, Johann Wolfgang; *Theory of Colours*
 (Cambridge: The MIT Press, 1970; reprint of the 1840
 C. L. Eastlake translation) · For the quote on page 9, see §135.

von Goethe, Johann Wolfgang; *Wilhem Meister*
 (Richmond: Alma Classics, 2020) · For Goethe's 'koan', see page 705.

Lagrange, Marc; *Senza Parole*
 (Munich: teNeues, 2016)

Nou, Jean-Louis and Louis Fréderic, *Borobudur*
 (New York: Abbeville Press, 1996) · The mention on page 18 is from
 the introductory essay 'Borobudur, Center of the Cosmos' (page 16).

Pande, Alke; *Flower Shower: the Culture of Flowers in India*
 (New Delhi: Niyogi Books, 2019)

Østergaard, Jan Stubbe; ' "Reconstruction" of the polychromy of
 ancient sculpture: a necessary evil?', *Techné*, Vol. 48, 2019

Wittgenstein, Ludwig; *Remarks on Colour*
 (Oxford: Blackwell, 1977). For the quote, see §70.

IMAGE CREDITS

p. 8 (left) *Grave monument of Phrasikleia, colour reconstruction*, 2010
 Polymethyl metacrylate, natural pigments. H: 200cm

 Liebieghaus Skulpturensammlung, Frankfurt, Polychromy Research Project,
 Frankfurt am Main, since 2014 loan from Ludwig-Maximilians-Universität München,
 Leibnizpreis 2007, O. Primavesi. Photo:© Liebieghaus Skulpturensammlung,
 Frankfurt am Main – Vinzenz Brinkmann – Ulrike Koch-Brinkmann – ARTOTHEK

p. 8 (right) *Statue of a woman wrapping herself in a cloak, so-called Little Herculan.* 2019
 Marble stucco on plaster cast; natural pigments in egg tempera; gold leaf, H: 185cm
 © Liebieghaus Skulpturensammlung, Frankfurt am Main – Vinzenz Brinkmann –
 Ulrike Koch-Brinkmann - ARTOTHEK

p. 20 Marc Lagrange: *Alto Rilievo*, 2015
 © Marc Lagrange, 2015 · Reproduced with permission

pp. 22-83 All artworks courtesy of John and Fausta Eskenazi.

pp. 23-82 All flowers courtesy of Auntie and her cortège.

COLOPHON

For art to have a civilizing effect on the course of human history, it must first be made; it then needs to be cherished and cultivated. It is rare to find two people who not only appreciate Indian and south-east Asian art, but who, through their diligence and knowledge, ensure that these great works retain their proper place in the grand scheme. Such are JOHNNY AND FAUSTA ESKENAZI, *and it has been my great privilege to enjoy their friendship and their generosity, evidenced in every page of this book.*

Puṣpa

A photographic essay in which cut flowers are coupled with Indian and south-east Asian sculptures and reliefs

© ORNAN ROTEM, 2021

No part of this publication may be reproduced in any form whatsoever without the prior written permission of the author or the publisher.

EDITORIAL: Mona Gainer-Salim
DESIGN: Ornan Rotem

Set in Eric Gill's Perpetua, first published by Monotype in 1929, a typeface patterned after epigraphic rather than calligraphic letters arising naturally from Gill's stone-cutter's skills; at the same time it is characterized by deep feeling for the structure and history of lettering.

Printed in the UK by Zone Graphics, on Mohawk Superfine and Fedrigoni Symbol Freelife

SYLPH EDITIONS · LONDON | 2021
ISBN 978-1-909631-38-0
www.sylpheditions.com